URGE TO
KILL

POLICE THE ILLUSTRATED NEWS

LAW COURTS AND WEEKLY RECORD

No. 1,292.   SATURDAY, NOVEMBER 17, 1888.   Price One Penny.

SKETCHES OF THE SEVENTH EAST END CRIME.

PHOTOGRAPHING THE BODY. — REMOVING THE BODY TO SHOREDITCH MORTUARY. — A MYSTERIOUS MAN WITH A BLACK BAG — FORCING OPEN THE DOOR

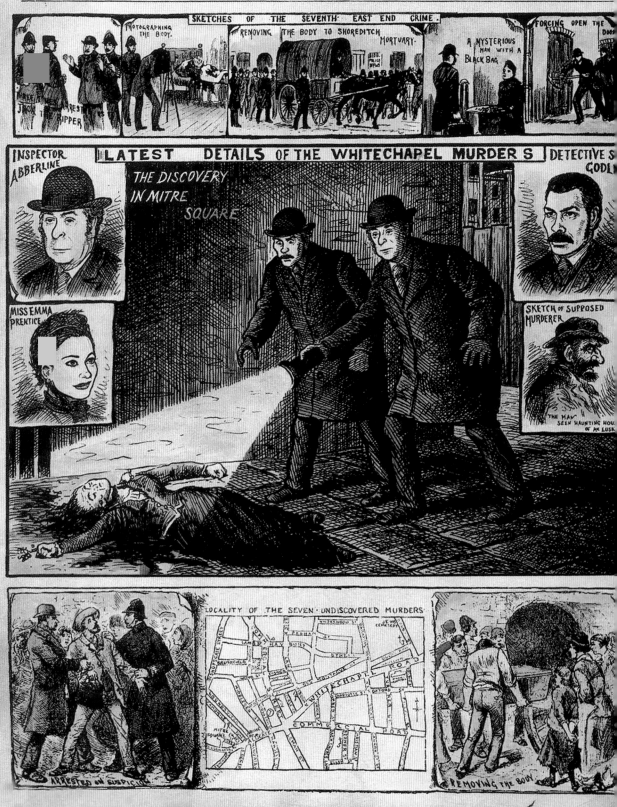

LATEST DETAILS OF THE WHITECHAPEL MURDERS

THE DISCOVERY IN MITRE SQUARE

INSPECTOR ABBERLINE

MISS EMMA PRENTICE

DETECTIVE SGT GODLEY

SKETCH OF SUPPOSED MURDERER

THE MAN SEEN HAUNTING HOUSE OF McLUSK

ARRESTED ON SUSPICION — LOCALITY OF THE SEVEN UNDISCOVERED MURDERS — REMOVING THE BODY

URGE TO
KILL

**How police take homicide
from case to court**

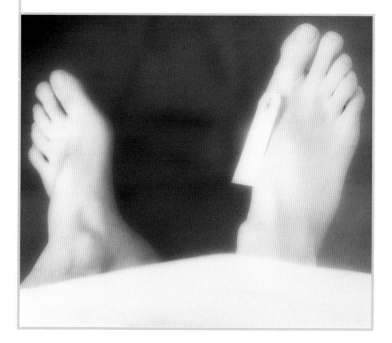

MARTIN EDWARDS

WRITER'S DIGEST BOOKS
CINCINNATI, OHIO
www.writersdigest.com

A QUINTET BOOK

First published in the United States in 2002 by Writer's Digest.

Distributed to the trade markets in North America by
Writer's Digest Books
an imprint of F&W Publications, Inc.
4700 East Galbraith Road
Cincinnati, OH 45236
(800) 289-0963

Library of Congress Cataloguing-in-Publication Data available

ISBN 1-58297-131-5

This book was conceived, designed and produced by
Quintet Publishing Limited
6 Blundell Street
London N7 7 BH

Creative Director: Richard Dewing
Project Editor and Picture Researcher: Toria Leitch
Managing Editor: Diana Steedman
Designer: James Lawrence

Manufactured in Singapore by Universal Graphics
Printed in China by Midas Printing

Picture credits

The publisher would like to thank the following for permission to reproduce their images. While every effort has been made to ensure this listing is correct the publisher apologises for any omissions or errors.

Topham Picturepoint
pp 2, 7, 9, 10, 17 (tr), 23 (t, bl), 27, 29, 31 (b), 32, 33, 35, 36, 47 (bl, br), 49 (tl, b), 55, 57, 62, 68, 69, 70, 73, 75, 79 (tr, bl, br), 81 (l), 85 (b), 87, 89 (tl), 91 (b), 95, 99, 101, 105, 109, 111 (br), 119 (tr, b), 124 (t), 125 (tr, b), 129, 131, 136 (b), 137 (tr, b), 142, 143 (tl, tr, bl), 147 (t, br), 149 (b), 154, 155 (tr, b), 159, 161 (br), 165, 167, 169, 171 (b), 175, 177, 181, 183 (t, bl), 185, 187 (t)

Science Photo Library
pp 3 (Cristina Pedrazzini), 8 (Peter Menzel), 15 (David Parker), 17 (tl: Michel Viard), 21 (Mauro Fermariello), 39 (Michel Viard), 45 (Chris Bjornberg), 55 (bl: Dr Jurgen Scriba), 91 (t: GJLP/CNRI), 112 (Peter Menzel), 115 (Peter Menzel), 121 (TEK IMAGE), 125 (tl: Dr Jurgen Scriba), 132 (Costantino Margiotta), 136 (t: Volker Steger), 155 (tl: Oscar Burriel), 161 (t: Geoff Tompkinson), 178 (Costantino Margiotta)

Frank Spooner
pp 11, 12, 23 (br), 25, 43 (bl, br), 49 (tr), 53, 59, 61, 65, 89 (tr, b), 93, 97, 111 (t), 124 (b), 147 (bl), 149 (t), 161 (bl), 163, 171 (t)

Atlantic Syndication Partners
pp 43, 63 (b), 66, 67, 85 (t), 143 (br)

Anglia Press Agency
pp 79 (tl), 119 (tl)

Wilfred Gregg
pp 17 (bl, br), 31 (t), 43 (t), 47 (t), 102, 137 (t), 173, 183 (br), 187 (bl)

The Toronto Star
p 103

Sirchi Fingerprint Laboratory
p 81 (tr)

CONTENTS

INTRODUCTION

Before my first mystery novel was published in 1991, I wrote legal textbooks. Those books needed to be accurate, but I believed from day one that if they were not also interesting to read, no one would stick around long enough to check their accuracy. My approach to this project reflects the need to strike a similar balance.

It is important nowadays, perhaps more than ever, that the factual background of a mystery novel be properly researched. If it contains too many glaring mistakes, the reader will return the book to the shelf but not return to the author. Crime writers and enthusiasts should treat Stephen Leadbeater's scathing essay "Forensic Pathologist" in *The Oxford Companion to Crime & Mystery Writing* (1999) as a warning of the traps that abound for the unwary. So care is needed, and one aim of this guide is to supply useful information, together with clues as to further areas of research. This will help readers, particularly those who plan to write a mystery novel, to skip around the pitfalls that abound in the field of homicide investigation and all its complexities.

> **"There's a scarlet thread of murder running through the colourless skein of life, and our duty is to unravel it, and isolate it, and expose every inch of it."**
>
> Sir Arthur Conan Doyle *A Study in Scarlet* (1887)

The book tours a broad array of subjects, taken from around the world: police and legal rules, motives, weapons, crime scene procedures and so on, together with links to real life cases and published crime fiction of today and yesterday. To take just one example, the small print of the statutory regulations that govern murder cases varies, sometimes widely, from one country to another and there are also differences in the laws of different states in the United States. I have tried to simplify, although I hope without undue distortion, the description of complex police procedures and technical forensic processes and have chosen appropriate material and case studies to illustrate this. Readers should treat this book as a starting point, a stimulus to more thorough study of a fascinating subject (a guide to sources of further information

Police monitor surveillance screens.

appears at the end of the book). Because of the pace of change in technology, many printed sources soon become out of date on some points, so it makes sense to supplement any research with excursions across the World Wide Web. In addition, writers frequently gain benefits from talking personally to law enforcement officers and forensic scientists. It is gratifying how busy specialists, if approached in a reasonable manner, freely give their time to help further our understanding of their complex procedures.

However, factual accuracy is not enough to guarantee success for a budding mystery novelist. A novel is, after all, a work of imagination, perhaps an opportunity for the reader

1 A forensic officer dusts for prints and searches for clues at the scene of a murder.
2 A police investigator in white overalls surveys the scene in a supermarket where armed officers shot dead a man who had taken the store manager hostage and held a knife to his throat.

to escape from his or her mundane life. If the novel becomes too bogged down in logistical small print, it will fail as a work of creative fiction, even if it functions adequately as an instruction manual. I have, therefore, tried to supply hints about a few of the areas that a would-be mystery writer may wish to explore for himself or herself in composing a well-realized piece of genre fiction. Freshness is crucial, as is an understanding of human character, including the motives that give someone the urge to kill. Ingenuity is, arguably, at the core of many of the classic crimes and imagination, coupled with empathy, certainly beats hardest in the heart of winning crime fiction.

In putting this book together I have been helped by many people, including representatives of law enforcement agencies and prosecution authorities, whose opinions and suggestions I have endeavored to incorporate. Speakers at crime writing conferences have added to my stock of knowledge. I have also read, both in researching this book and over many years, countless books on true crime and mystery novels. Like any other author in the field, I have built gratefully on the work of my predecessors. My apologies are humbly submitted to the authors of any influential works that I have omitted, through lapse of memory or lack of space. My special thanks go to the following: Peter and Rhoda Walker, who supplied me with much valuable information about the contemporary investigative process from the police perspective; Douglas Huke and Joan Lock, both knowledgeable writers on true crime; my agent Mandy Little for keeping the faith; all those at Quintet who have worked on this book; and, above all, to my long-suffering family, who endured, with their usual good humor, a few months of seeing their home swamped by the literature of murder most foul.

Martin Edwards

1 Police investigators photograph and search the sectioned off area of a crime scene.
2 Officers search the ruins of a burnt-out house where the remains of a body were found.

CHAPTER ONE

MURDER BASICS

> **"Justice cannot reach all wrongs; its hands are tied by the restrictions of the law."**
>
> Melville Davisson Post,
> *The Strange Schemes of Randolph Mason* (1896)

Murder itself is a category of homicide. And homicide is where a person directly or indirectly causes the death of another human being. Homicides may be culpable, for example, in cases of murder, manslaughter, infanticide, and criminal negligence. Homicides may also be nonculpable, such as where the killing is in self-defense or is wholly accidental.

WHAT IS MURDER?

The legal definition of murder is not uniform throughout the world, but murder essentially occurs when a person intended to cause the death of another; to cause bodily harm that was likely to lead to death; or set out to cause the death of one person but killed someone else.

The United States and many other countries recognize two degrees of murder; the United Kingdom recognizes a single crime of murder, always punishable by life imprisonment. In both first-degree murder (murder one) and second-degree murder (murder two), there must be an intention to kill. The difference between first-degree and second-degree murder does not lie in the scale of violence used, but rather in the circumstances of the case. First-degree murder is planned and deliberate, or committed during the course of certain offenses (such as abduction or

Mortuary technicians place a male human body into a mobile cold storage facility.

Previous page: The murder scene of a Mafia killing. The markings indicate the original position of the victim after the shooting.

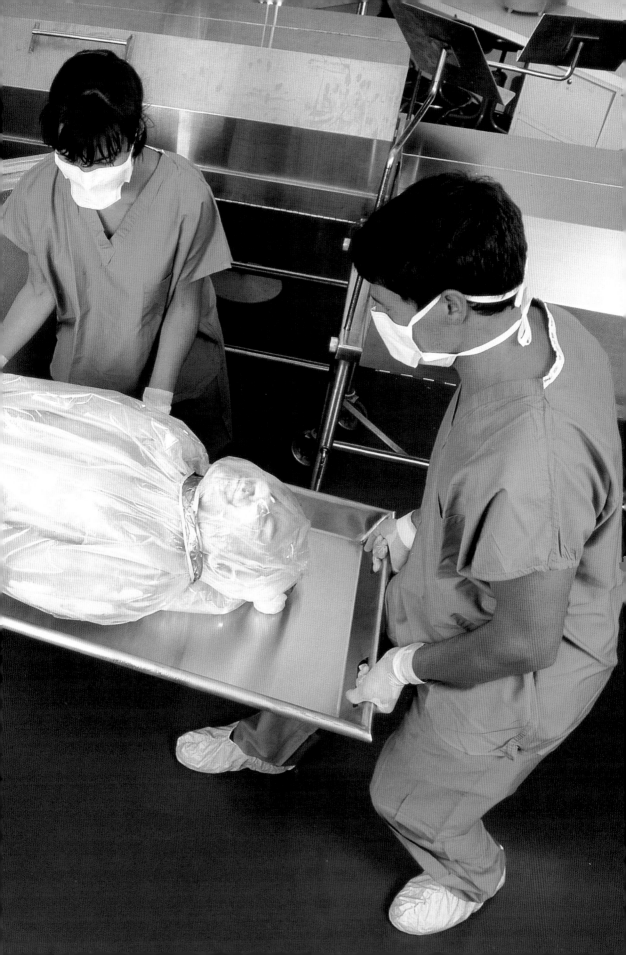

rape), or the murder of specified law enforcement officers in the line of duty. Murders falling outside that definition—which again is not uniform in every jurisdiction—are classified as second-degree murder. A charge of manslaughter is appropriate in a case of culpable homicide where there is no adequate proof of intention to cause death.

Diminished capacity or responsibility for a killing, or insanity, give rise to problems that are treated in various ways throughout the world. Even within the U.S., the legal definition of insanity is not precisely the same in every state. Particular problems arise in cases where the outlandish or horrific nature of the killing suggests that the culprit must have been insane and disagreements frequently arise between expert psychiatric witnesses called by the prosecution and defense respectively. The impression made by expert testimony, if guilt is proven, may influence both the verdict on the charge and the sentence.

AUTOMATISM

The courts in most countries tend to be skeptical of a defense to a murder charge based on automatism. The defense may involve insane automatism, typically where the murderer was suffering an epileptic episode when the crime took place. Jack Ruby, the Dallas nightclub operator who killed Lee Harvey Oswald, President John F. Kennedy's assassin, in 1963, was said by defense psychiatrists to be afflicted by psychomotor epilepsy at the time of the killing, but he was nevertheless found guilty of murder. In 1926, Lock Ah Tam, a Chinese man living in Liverpool, England, was hanged for shooting his wife and daughters, despite a powerful defense argument based on epilepsy and automatism; today the case would be treated as one of diminished responsibility. On the other hand, non-insane automatism may involve a crime committed while sleepwalking, as happened in 1987 when Ken Parks of Toronto, Canada, killed his mother-in-law and gravely injured her husband. He was found not guilty of murder, but acquittals on this basis remain rare.

CONSPIRACY

A conspiracy to murder arises when two or more people agree to commit the crime. Although laws vary in their detail from country to country, it is generally the case that a person who solicits a murder is treated as being the person who actually kills the victim. Conspiracies often arise in gangland disputes: Murder Inc., the Mafia's gun-for-hire service of 1930s New York, is a classic example. Conspiracies are also common in domestic crimes, for example where a pair of lovers agree to murder the spouse or partner of one or other of them. Recent years have seen a steady increase in the number of crimes attributed to contract killings, that is, where a person is paid to commit murder while the instigator takes care to establish an unbreakable alibi for the time of death. A common mistake is incompetence in the choice of hired killer. A typical example arose in Clinton, Oklahoma, in 1992, when Linda Ponce allegedly conspired with a former husband to kill her current husband. Her error was to engage the services of an undercover cop to perform the task.

1 Forensic laboratory examination of residues of explosive on materials found at a crime scene.
2 Jack Ruby walks through the Dallas city jail, accused of firing a fatal bullet into the abdomen of Lee Oswald who assassinated President Kennedy.
3 Ian Brady, of the Moors murdering couple from 1960s Britain.
4 Myra Hindley, Ian Brady's partner in crime.

The dividing line between conspiracy to murder and folie à deux is often difficult to draw. The latter is best described as an insanity shared between two people who independently might never have committed murder but who together form a lethal partnership. It may arise in varying circumstances. Famous homicidal female partnerships include the New Zealand teenagers Pauline Parker and Juliet Hume, who killed Pauline's mother in 1954; and the French sisters Christine and Lee Papin, who murdered their employer in 1933. The Leopold and Loeb case in Chicago in 1924, and the similar British case of Richard Elsey and Jamie Petrolini in 1994, saw pairs of polite students from affluent backgrounds killing as an experimental exercise. Murderous man-woman combinations recall Martha Beck and Raymond Fernandez, the American Lonely Hearts Killers of the 1940s, and Britain's Ian Brady and Myra Hindley, another pair of serial killers who committed the Moors Murders in the 1960s. There is almost always a strong sexual component in folie à deux cases, but the phenomenon is still inadequately understood and it does not in itself provide a defense to a charge of murder.

CRIME PASSIONNEL

Crime passionnel is a French term meaning "crime of passion." There is a mistaken popular view, outside of France, that this means a person can kill a lover in a passionate rage and be acquitted. In France the legal profession makes a formal acknowledgment of the power of love and jealousy. But *crime passionnel* is not a formal plea. The question for the court is simply whether the murder was premeditated, though the state of mind of the murderer will form part of their judgment. A crime of passion will usually rank as second-degree murder in the U.S. The case of Jean Harris and the Scarsdale Diet Doctor killing of 1980 (see pages 18-19) is a classic example.

THE ANATOMY OF A MURDER INVESTIGATION

A murder inquiry can be divided into five main but closely inter-linked stages. The first is the initial police response and priority police actions. In any case of homicide, the initial action proceeds on the basis that the case might involve a murder, until the investigation proves otherwise. Preservation of evidence at the crime scene is crucial. The second is the analysis of the crime and the development of a strategy. The third is the analysis of the crime on the basis of factual evidence, including sound theorizing. The fourth involves carrying out suspect inquiries: assessment of the modus operandi (method of operation or MO) of the culprit; analysis of crime scene evidence; and collecting data from informants and forensic material. Last comes the disposal of the case. Even when a suspect has been charged, the investigation must carry on, producing a timeline for the suspect's movements and assessing possible links with other crimes. Investigators must also be ready to resume work should the person accused of the crime be acquitted.

The key issues that typically challenge a homicide investigation team are:

- **Who has been killed?**
- **How?**
- **Where?**
- **When?**
- **Why?**
- **By whom?**

The answers to some of these questions may be available immediately; others will determine whether a conviction can be secured.

Effective assessment of the crime scene requires analysis of information not only about the scene itself, but also about the victim and the offender. Forensic information gathered at the scene and through an autopsy of the victim helps to generate lines of inquiry. Investigators need to look at patterns of behavior for both the offender and the victim that might prove relevant to the crime. Developing a psychological profile of the offender may also contribute to the formation of theories guiding the direction of initial inquiries.

Locard's Principle, named for the French forensic scientist Edmond Locard, states that "Every contact leaves a trace." Forensic science combines this with scientific methodology, providing a crucial interpretation of scientific information in the context of the individual circumstances of each crime. Forensic science is context-sensitive: to obtain the best forensic information, the scientist must be able to evaluate information in the full context of the crime. It is crucial, therefore, for investigators to work in close liaison with forensic scientists and communicate fully with advisers so that information can be provided to detectives without delay.

FORENSIC INVESTIGATION

A forensic pathologist seeks to determine some or all of the following:

- the identity of the deceased
- the time of death
- the manner of death (natural causes, accident, suicide, or homicide)
- the cause of death

Forensic pathologists generally have a broad working knowledge in various forensic areas, in addition to traditional fields such as toxicology, ballistics, trace evidence, forensic serology, and DNA profiling. The forensic pathologist is, in effect, the case coordinator for the medical and forensic assessment of the death, seeking to ensure that appropriate procedures and techniques for gathering evidence are followed.

In states where there is a medical examiner system, a forensic pathologist is usually employed to perform autopsies (post mortems) to establish the cause of death. Forensic pathologists in the U.S. may work for private hospitals, cities, counties, states, the military services, or the federal government.

The forensic pathologist's work often begins at the crime scene. His or her task is simplified if the medical history of the deceased and cause of death are available. Before undertaking an autopsy, the forensic pathologist begins by examining the body externally. Later, during the course of an autopsy, various laboratory tests may be undertaken to provide further clues. In the light of all the information gained, the forensic pathologist should be able to form a view as to the cause and manner of death and to prepare a report detailing the findings. Usually, the forensic pathologist will be required to give evidence in court to explain his or her findings and how they were reached.

A coroner is a public official, appointed or elected in a particular jurisdiction, whose job is to hold an inquest into deaths in certain circumstances. In many states in the U.S. the tradition of electing coroners, sometimes with little relevant expertise, has given way to the appointment of a medical examiner. A medical examiner is a physician charged with investigating

THEN AND NOW

BLOOD EVIDENCE

The blood spilled in a homicide case can provide investigators with vital clues. Even where a murderer has gone to great lengths to clean up the crime scene, it is all too easy for a small trace of blood to be left that may be found and tested. The science of serology (the analysis of the properties and effects of serums such as blood) developed from very unsophisticated beginnings. In 1869, a French detective named Gustave Macé could find no obvious traces of blood in a room where he believed a victim had been dismembered. Macé poured water on the floor tiles and, when the tiles were taken up, their under-surfaces were caked in dried blood, thus leading to a confession from the prime suspect.

Although different types of blood were identified in the nineteenth century, it was not until the beginning of the twentieth that Dr. Karl Landsteiner standardized the identification of types, taking into account that red blood cells contain substances known as antigens, which produce antibodies to combat infection. The types were classified by reference to the presence or absence of two antigens (A and B), into four groups: A, B, O, and AB. A and O are the commonest and AB (with both antigens present) is the rarest. This represented an important step forward in crime detection, since if blood belonging to type A is found on clothing worn by a suspect who has type O blood, then the blood traces must come from someone else. If the victim had type A blood, then it is possible (but not certain) that the blood came from the victim. Later, it was discovered that about eighty percent of human beings are secretors, that is, their other body fluids contain the same substances as their blood and so can be used to determine blood type.

An Italian, Dr. Leon Lattes, discovered how to apply blood testing to stains on material, by using a saline solution, and how to test for antibodies in dried blood. In 1949, the British scientists Barr and Bertram found that the nuclei of male and female body cells could be distinguished—this effect was most notable in white blood cells, thus providing an additional means of identification through blood samples.

Despite steady advances in serology, crime investigations can be seriously compromised by procedural flaws at a crime scene. When Dr. Sam Sheppard's wife was found dead in Cleveland, Ohio in 1954, blood evidence at the scene was inadequately examined. Sheppard was convicted but eventually released following more skilful interpretation of the blood evidence. Following the disappearance of her baby daughter Azaria, near Ayers Rock in Australia in 1980, Lindy Chamberlain was convicted of murder, but released after it emerged that blood evidence had been misinterpreted.

DNA profiling has given serology a new dimension, since matching DNA from a blood sample at the scene to a source provides more accurate results than drawing up a blood profile in the way pioneered by Landsteiner. But in the 1995 murder trial of O. J. Simpson, the defense argued that the control samples of blood found at the scene and alleged to match Simpson's DNA had been contaminated in the crime labs. The case illustrates the need for careful handling of evidence, and the importance of explaining the significance of that evidence clearly and convincingly when the case eventually comes to court.

A geneticist examines a DNA autoradiogram showing a genetic sequence analysis created on film.

and examining cases where someone dies a sudden, unexpected, or violent death. In contrast to a traditional coroner lacking medical qualifications, the medical examiner brings professional expertise to the assessment of the medical history and physical examination of the body. Often, the medical examiner will be a forensic pathologist. In England and Wales there is no direct equivalent to the medical examiner system and coroners are either qualified lawyers or medical practitioners. In Scotland the duties of a coroner are performed by the Procurator-Fiscal.

POLICE

The Federal Bureau of Investigation (FBI) is the chief investigative arm of the U.S. Department of Justice. It is not the same as a national police force. It has a broad investigative mandate but does not determine whether a person will be prosecuted; federal prosecutors are responsible for that decision and for conducting the prosecution.

The FBI employs over 11,000 highly trained special agents. There is often some misunderstanding about the powers of special agents. Wiretapping, for instance, is strictly controlled by federal statutes. Deadly force may be used only when necessary, perhaps where the special agent has reason to believe that the subject of such force poses an imminent threat of death or serious injury to the special agent or someone else. If feasible, a verbal warning to submit to the special agent's authority must be given prior to the use of deadly force.

State and local law enforcement agencies are not subordinate to the FBI. However, the investigative resources of those agencies and the FBI are often combined to investigate and solve cases, and task forces of special agents and state and local officers are quite commonplace, especially in dealing with organized crime, bank robbery, kidnaping, or terrorism. Training for local law enforcement officers is available at the FBI National Academy at Quantico, Virginia.

Technical law enforcement systems in the U.S., as elsewhere, are increasingly sophisticated. The Integrated Automated Fingerprint Identification System (IAFIS) was introduced in 1999 to replace the previous paper-based system for identifying and searching criminal records. It supports a law enforcement agency's ability to record fingerprints and electronically exchange information with the FBI. The National Crime Information Center (NCIC) is a computerized index of documented criminal justice data available to law enforcement agencies. NCIC maintains a missing persons file, which lists over 100,000 people. The FBI's Critical Incident Response Group (CIRG) provides rapid assistance in the event of crisis, from the abduction or mysterious disappearance of children to hostage negotiation.

In England and Wales the Home Secretary, a senior politician, is ultimately responsible for the Metropolitan Police Force in London and has overall political power in relation to national policing matters. Local police authorities (the members of which include elected local politicians) run local policing and appoint the Chief Constable of the force. The Chief Constable is, however, guaranteed freedom from political

1 Forensic scientists inspect a scene where a murder has taken place in Nottingham, England.
2 A police forensic officer removes evidence from the burnt-out shell of a private cinema in central London. Eight people died in the blaze, which was thought to have been started deliberately.
3 An officer from the FBI academy.

influence in exercising his executive function. There are forty-three local police forces in England and Wales, but various national services have been created, including Regional Crime Squads and the National Criminal Intelligence Service (NCIS), which coordinates information about the most serious crimes and offenders.

Interpol was established in 1923 and now has its headquarters in Lyons, France. Its aim is to promote mutual assistance between police forces in different countries, overcoming national boundaries that may—especially in today's shrinking world—impede the fight against crime, while fully respecting the sovereignty of each nation. A key objective is to ensure its member states have a rapid, reliable, secure, and permanently available system for transmitting information to each other. A crime such as murder often becomes international because the offender commits the murder in one country and takes refuge in another. Interpol provides the machinery to ensure that the existence of national boundaries does not impede the course of justice.

THE CRIMINAL JUSTICE SYSTEM

Common law criminal justice systems found in the U.S., Canada, England, Australia, and various other English-speaking jurisdictions adopt an adversarial approach to the criminal process. The main responsibility for presenting evidence and legal arguments lies with the prosecuting authority, not with the judge. The accused is presumed to be innocent and the onus of proving guilt is on the prosecution. In continental European jurisdictions, much of Latin America, and parts of Africa and Asia, the civil law system usually prevails, favoring the inquisitorial approach. This involves a continuing investigation,

first by the police and later by an examining magistrate with broad authority. The examining magistrate directs the evidence gathering process, questions witnesses, and interrogates suspects. If the examining magistrate decides that there is evidence of guilt the case proceeds to trial and the onus is on the accused to refute the case against him.

The U.S. has a federal system, with power split between a central authority and states or local authorities. Each state has a criminal procedure law, as does the federal government, and the procedures adopted vary, although there are many similarities in fundamentals. A person prosecuted in a particular state court is subject to the criminal procedure applied in that state, and it is possible for state law to provide more extensive rights for a defendant than are guaranteed by the U.S. Constitution.

Safeguards are built into criminal justice systems to protect the civil rights of people caught up in an enquiry. Detectives need to comply with a variety of rules in order to avoid giving a prime suspect legal grounds on which to escape conviction. It is not up to detectives to determine the guilt or innocence of a person charged: that is a matter for the court. The detectives' job is to ensure that the preparation of the case is fair and unbiased. Any evidence in favor of the accused should be presented so that lawyers for the defense can use it.

An important and time-consuming task for detectives is to compile a file of evidence for presentation at court. Preparing this file requires meticulous care. Knowledge of the legal rules of evidence is also essential; detectives need to be aware of what evidence the court will or will not be able to take into account when deciding on the

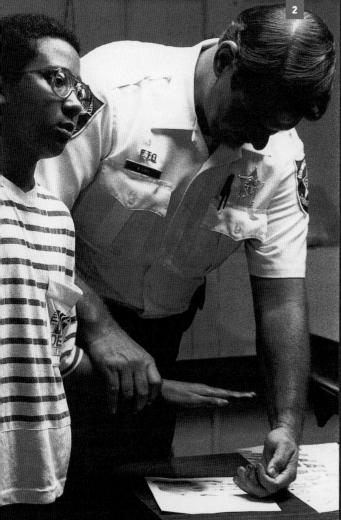

1 SWAT officers—for special weapons and tactics—arrest a suspect in conjunction with drugs and violence charges in Florida's seedier side of Miami.
2 A juvenile is being fingerprinted as part of the booking procedure.

verdict. In general, most courts will allow witnesses to give evidence only about matters perceived through their own senses, but there are some exceptions to this principle. For instance, a dying declaration by a murder victim about the cause of his or her fatal injuries is sometimes treated as admissible evidence.

Before a suspect is questioned in custody, the police must issue a warning informing him or her of various legal rights. In the U.S. the Miranda Warning reminds suspects of their rights—for instance that they have the right to remain silent but that anything they say may be used against them in a court of law. Miranda Rights are, therefore, largely a protection against self-incrimination; they offer no protection against arrest. To make an arrest, the police simply need to have probable cause—a sufficient reason—based on facts and observations, to believe that the suspect has committed a crime. The Miranda Warning should be given prior to interrogation since, if it is not, a judge may refuse to allow the court to consider any statements made by the suspect, even if the arrest itself was valid.

What happens to a suspect who has been taken into custody varies from country to country, but the procedure in the U.S. is typical. A suspect will first be booked and an administrative record made of the arrest. Booking may also involve searching, fingerprinting, and photographing the suspect. In a homicide case the suspect may be required to await the filing of the initial charge document—which must take place within a reasonable time—before appearing in front of a judge or magistrate. Usually, the magistrate will assess the evidence to ensure that probable cause has been established and bail may be granted. Bail is generally unavailable, however, for people charged with offenses that could result in the death penalty.

In many states in the U.S., a person must be indicted, that is, formally charged by a grand jury before the trial. Other states convene a preliminary hearing. The question for the grand jury or presiding judge is whether there is sufficient probable cause to justify continuing the proceedings. Generally, the grand jury hears only the evidence submitted by the prosecution and the accused does not have the right to be present, to submit evidence, or to cross-examine witnesses for the prosecution. An arraignment takes place in the court in which the accused is to be tried. The accused has to answer the charge, for example by pleading not guilty.

Key components of a jury trial are usually:

- **jury selection**
- **opening statements by prosecution and defense attorneys**
- **evidence (first presented by the prosecution, then by the defense) and questioning of witnesses**
- **closing arguments of prosecution and defense attorneys**
- **the judge's summing-up according to the relevant law**
- **the jury's verdict**
- **the sentence of the court**

There are three categories of witnesses who may give evidence: the lay witness is someone who can tell the court anything that has relevance to the case; the expert witness will have professional qualifications and experience that justify his or her expressing an opinion on a point after considering information available; and the professional witness is a law enforcement officer who has been trained to observe, record, and present evidence (including dealing with cross-examination from defense lawyers, which is often extremely hostile). Detectives need to cooperate closely with the prosecution legal team to anticipate lines of attack on the case against the accused. This may, for example, involve detailed discussions about the strength of expert evidence—typically on forensic material—that is to be put before the court, and the development of a strategy for presenting the evidence so as to minimize the risk that it will not stand up to close scrutiny.

A hung jury is one unable to agree on its verdict. Some states require the verdict to be unanimous, while others permit a majority verdict. If the jury cannot reach a verdict, the defendant may be retried before another jury.

Following a guilty verdict, the convicted defendant may seek a new trial on the basis that the conduct of the trial was prejudicial, perhaps on the grounds that the judge's direction on the admissibility of evidence was in error.

The operations room of the Bedfordshire CID, as police continue the murder hunt for the "A6" killer of Valerie Storie.

CORONERS AND MEDICAL EXAMINERS

The judicial office of coroner is generally regarded as unique to England and countries that were once under English rule, although some researchers trace a version of the coroner's main function of investigating the cause of death back to the Tang and Song dynasties of ancient China. The origins in England of the office of coroner are uncertain, although it probably dates back to the ninth century and the time of King Alfred the Great. The statutory regime for coroners began in the twelfth century, during the reign of King Richard I, when the Articles of Eyres stated that the "keepers of the pleas" of the Crown would look after the King's interests in local affairs. The original coroners were elected, land-owning knights.

Historically, the coroner had a wide variety of duties. They were, for example, expected to attend a trial by ordeal—which might involve walking over red-hot ploughshares or holding red-hot coals for nine paces—and record the outcome. In an attempt to stamp out trial by battle, coroners were given the power to hear private prosecutions if the Crown did not take up a case. They also had jurisdiction over "treasure trove," that is, gold or silver in the form of coins, bullion, or plate that had been deliberately hidden by the owner.

Whoever discovered a dead body had a duty to raise the "hue and cry." The four nearest households had to be alerted to begin the hunt for the killer and the coroner also had to be informed. The locals were required to guard the body until the coroner arrived to inquire into the death—the origin of the term "inquest." If the body was moved, the community suffered financial penalties. The duty to advise the coroner survives to this day and a body should not be interfered with unless a coroner permits it.

The election of coroners was abolished in the nineteenth century and the nature of their work has changed somewhat. Today, coroners are medically or legally qualified and their main duties are to determine the medical cause of death, to allay rumor or suspicion, to draw attention to circumstances that might lead to further deaths, to advance medical knowledge, and to preserve the legal interests of the deceased's family and heirs. The range of deaths that must be reported to the coroner include those where the cause cannot readily be identified as natural and where there are suspicious circumstances. In some cases, for example where death occurred in a way that may affect public health and safety, the coroner must summon a jury to assist at the inquest. The inquest will determine the identity of the deceased, the date and place of death, and the manner of death. A jury can return a verdict of unlawful killing, but in England it cannot name an individual as guilty. The last person to be named as guilty by an English coroner's jury was Lord Lucan, who disappeared following the murder of his children's nanny Sandra Rivett in 1975 and has never since been found.

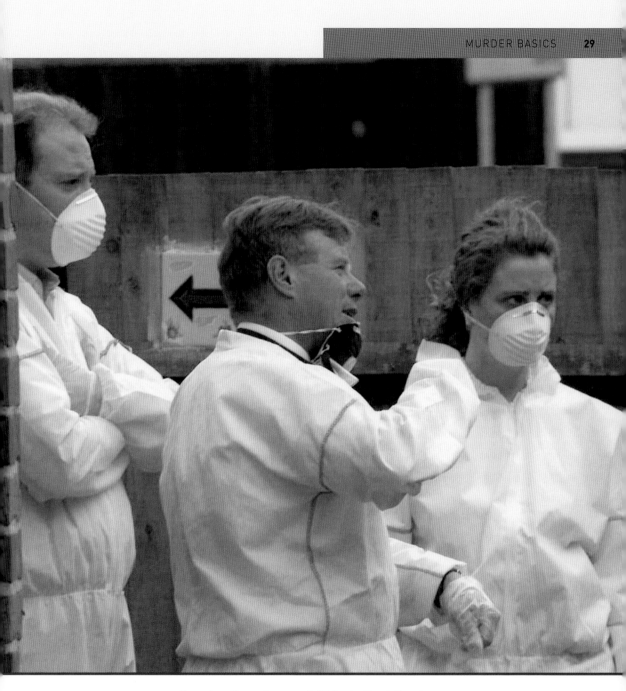

Forensic police at the scene in Wellesley Road, Slough,
England, where two men and a woman were found murdered.

In the U.S., the office of coroner has been replaced in many states by that of the medical examiner.
Early on, American coroners were allowed to charge for their services, unlike their English counterparts—
a tradition that fostered corruption. The office of coroner, where it is retained, remains a political post.
Medical examiners are pathologists capable of carrying out post mortems and are usually appointed by the
state. Their expertise plays a vital part in the detection of many homicides.

MAD OR BAD?

The serial killings of John Wayne Gacy raise certain questions about the sanity of a serial killer that, unfortunately, his trial did little to resolve. Gacy was an up-and-coming twenty-six-year-old businessman in Iowa when, in 1968, a friend's son accused him of sexual abuse. Police investigations revealed other victims, and Gacy pleaded guilty to sodomy and was sentenced to ten years in prison. His behavior in jail was excellent and he was paroled after only eighteen months.

Gacy moved to Chicago in 1971 and set up his own construction business. He was well-liked in the community as an enthusiastic hospital volunteer and children's entertainer. Yet in January 1972 he stabbed a young man he had picked up and buried the corpse in the crawlspace under his house. Less than six months later he married (for the second time), but the couple divorced in 1976, by which time Gacy had killed an employee, John Butkovich, and buried him in the crawlspace. The thirst for the sexual pleasure that murdering young men gave him was now insatiable and he started killing relentlessly. In December 1978, a fifteen-year-old named Robert Piest was reported missing by his parents after visiting Gacy to talk about a job. Police questioning received a flat denial from Gacy that he had ever met the boy. Nevertheless, Gacy was arrested at his home and police noticed a smell coming from the heating duct in his house. No fewer than twenty-nine bodies were found under the floor and a further four were found dumped in a nearby river.

There was no doubt that Gacy was a serial killer. The question at his trial was whether the court would accept that he was insane. He had spent six years sleeping above his victims' bodies and, from the start of his examination by psychiatrists, he insisted that he was prey to an evil alter-ego called Bad Jack, who was responsible for the crimes. Gacy was undoubtedly intelligent and capable of exuding personal charm; he liked to receive the admiration and respect of others and was proud of a photograph taken of himself with Rosalynn Carter, wife of the then-President. His claim that he had four personalities was not supported by compelling evidence, but another claim, that many of his murders were sparked by quarrels, may well have been true. He had a need to impose his will on others and felt no compunction in killing someone who challenged his authority; nor did he later show remorse. Defense psychiatrists related Gacy's abnormal behavior to a dysfunctional family background; his sadism was portrayed as a kind of reaction against his bullying alcoholic father. A psychiatric expert called by the prosecution disputed that Gacy could have had thirty-three cases of temporary insanity. The fact that he persuaded two young men to dig graves in the crawlspace was strong evidence of cold premeditation and the jury took a mere two hours to decide that Gacy was not mad, just bad. He was sentenced to death and executed by lethal injection.

1 John Wayne Gacy dressed as a clown before taking on a role as a children's entertainer.
2 Taken in 1972, this picture shows Gacy after the wedding to his second wife, Carole Hoff.

PASSION, DEPRESSION, OBSESSION

In 1980, Jean Harris and Dr. Herman Tarnower had been lovers for fourteen years. Tarnower was a cardiologist, an eminent and charismatic figure who devised the Scarsdale Diet. His book about the diet, published a year earlier, became a bestseller: in it he acknowledged Jean Harris's assistance with the research and writing. He also gave her four thousand U.S. dollars, but she wrote to him saying that she would have preferred a holiday with him.

Tarnower was strongly attracted to women, but at the age of sixty nine he had never married. He preferred to keep his lovers at a distance, and although he proposed marriage to Harris early in their relationship, this never occurred. Harris, a fifty-seven-year old divorcee and head teacher at a highly regarded school in Virginia, was aware that Tarnower had several affairs with other women, including a long-term liaison with Lynn Tryforos, the nurse-receptionist at the Scarsdale Clinic. Harris remained devoted to her lover, but he was tiring of her and invited Lynn Tryforos, rather than Harris, to accompany him to a prestigious dinner.

Harris had been having problems at work and suffered from depression. She finalized her will, sent a vitriolic letter to Tarnower, called him to say she would drive from Virginia to New York to see him, packed a .32 revolver and ammunition in her car, and set off. Upon arriving at Tarnower's house in Westchester County, she roused him from bed and a quarrel ensued. Harris found Lynn Tryforos's night clothes and curlers and threw them out a window. Tarnower slapped her, at which point she took the gun out of her bag and put it to her own head. Tarnower tried to take the gun from her. but in the struggle she fired, fatally wounding him. She was arrested at the scene.

Harris was charged with second-degree murder, implying intention to kill but no premeditation. The prosecutors were clearly aware that, in the circumstances, there was little or no chance of persuading a jury to treat the killing as a case of murder in the first degree. Harris's defense team argued that she had intended to kill herself, rather than Tarnower, whose death was said to be a tragic accident. The defense also put in evidence about Harris's downward spiral of depression and brought forward witnesses who testified to her character and integrity. Harris behaved with dignity throughout the trial, but she made no show of remorse and her evidence about the circumstances of the killing was unconvincing. The contents of the aggressive and paranoid "Scarsdale Letter" that she had sent to Tarnower seem to have played a crucial part in the jury's decision that she had a credible motive for murder and had killed Tarnower deliberately. Having been found guilty of second-degree murder, she was sentenced to fifteen years-to-life without parole.

Jean Harris is brought into the Harrison, N.Y. court where she was arraigned for the murder of Dr. Herman Tarnower.

PUBLIC ENEMY NO. 1

Few criminals have relished the limelight as much as Jacques Mesrine, a brazen robber, kidnaper, and killer whom the media dubbed France's Public Enemy No. 1. Born in 1936, Mesrine grew up during the German occupation, and after the war he served with distinction in the French army in Algeria. His military service over, he worked undercover for a sinister group dedicated to preserving French colonial control of Algeria, from which he learned the shooting skills and elusiveness which were to be a feature of his criminal career.

Mesrine craved excitement and satisfied it through crime. In 1961 he was convicted of robbery and firearms offenses and sent to prison. Following his release, he resumed a pattern of daring thefts, carried out with the assistance of his accomplice and lover Jeanne Schneider. The couple traveled to Canada where they graduated to kidnaping. In 1969, following a jail break, they were tried for the murder of a wealthy widow; although acquitted on that charge, they were returned to prison on kidnaping charges. Mesrine again escaped from prison and, with another convict on the run, murdered two forest rangers who got in their way. Returning to France, but with Interpol now on his trail, Mesrine became ever more audacious. After committing more armed robberies, he was captured by police but again escaped. The cycle repeated itself and, following a siege at his hideout, Mesrine was arrested once more.

Three and a half years passed before Mesrine's case came to court, a delay that illustrates the contrast between the inquisitorial system of justice in continental Europe and the adversarial process in jurisdictions such as the U.S., the U.K., Canada, and Australia. In France, the examining magistrate controls the investigation, with powers to order searches, seize private property, and summon and interrogate witnesses. A benefit of this system is that it restricts the opportunities for malpractice or incompetence on the part of the police by involving the judiciary at an early stage. But the downside is that a person can be held throughout the investigation and detainees who have not been convicted thus form a relatively high percentage of those in custody.

Mesrine was a flamboyant and impatient man and the long wait for his trial increased his hatred of the French legal machine. The judge, Charles Petit, was unsurprisingly hostile toward the accused and sentenced him to twenty years in prison. But a year later, true to form, Mesrine managed to break out of jail yet again. He was involved in a shoot-out in Normandy and a bank robbery, before attempting to kidnap Charles Petit—partly out of revenge and partly through a desire to make a dramatic statement about his contempt for French justice and its prison system. The audacious plan failed and massive resources were devoted to a manhunt for the arch-criminal. He was tracked down to a building in Montmartre; when he and his latest mistress emerged, police marksmen shot him dead. The legal establishment had taken its revenge on the man who had so often mocked it.

After being hunted for a long time, Jacques Mesrine was finally killed by officials of the Central Office against Banditism on the edge of Paris.

CHAPTER TWO

MEANS TO MURDER

"And now we know How, we know Who."

Dorothy L. Sayers, *Busman's Honeymoon* (1937)

A homicide investigation team needs to establish how death occurred. The first question is whether the homicide is culpable or not. The only safe assumption to make is to "think murder," and not assume too quickly that a death that appears to have resulted from some other cause has in fact done so. Where it is clear that murder has been committed, it is vital to determine how. Failure to do so may delay or prevent the identification of the killer. Even where police know who the culprit is, lack of proof about the precise means of murder may make it difficult, perhaps even impossible, to secure a conviction in court.

Guns and knives are, statistically, the most common murder weapons. But there are many other methods that a resourceful villain—and crime writer—may credibly exploit. The means used by murderers are infinitely varied, and range from crude to highly elaborate. The advantage of choosing a sophisticated method is that it may enable the killer to escape detection altogether. In some cases of poisoning, for example, no one may know that murder has even been committed. Dr. Harold Shipman of Hyde, England, poisoned and disposed of an unknown number of his patients

A ballistics expert shoots a machine gun in a firing range during research to determine whether the gun was used in a crime.

Previous page: A discarded bullet case lies in a pool of blood at Hanover Square in London on 9 August 2001, following a shooting incident in the early hours of the morning.

over many years while continuing to be regarded as a caring medical practitioner and a pillar of the community.

A murderer who opts for an ingenious method nevertheless takes a considerable risk. Once the plan begins to unravel, it is often obvious that only one person could have committed the crime. Although Shipman has never admitted his guilt, it seemed inconceivable to observers at his trial that any jury faced with the circumstantial and forensic evidence could fail to convict. The only reasonable area of doubt about the case concerns how many of his deceased patients would have lived but for his intervention. Other seemingly clever murder methods have often backfired upon their perpetrators. In Germany in 1992, Karl Kasper electrocuted his wife and claimed the death was an accident that occurred during a sex game. The court did not believe him and he received a twelve-year sentence.

Crime writers often build their stories around ingenious devices, occasionally with too much elaboration to sustain credibility. In the past, bullets and daggers made from ice were surprisingly plentiful in mystery fiction: this fashion was inaugurated by Anna Katherine Green, the first American woman to become a best-selling crime writer. Her novel *Initials Only* (1911) featured a small icicle shot from a pistol. Edgar Wallace offered a variation on the theme in *The Three Just Men* (1925), where lethal snake venom is frozen into tiny darts and fired from a fake cigarette holder with an insulated chamber used as a blowpipe.

The importance of detecting the method of murder was highlighted in a number of Dorothy L. Sayers' books, including *Busman's Honeymoon* (1937), which has a final chapter entitled "When You Know How, You Know Who." The murder method is a contraption that requires split-second timing to achieve success. The potential weakness of such a scheme is that it may test the reader's credulity. In *Unnatural Death* (1927), Sayers' murderer killed people by injecting air into them, a method that is highly unreliable in practice. In a 1949 mercy killing case, Dr. Herman Sander was put on trial for murder after injecting 40cc of air into a cancer patient in New Hampshire. He said that the patient was already dead at the time he injected the air, which he did "just to make sure." He was acquitted.

THE PERFECT MURDER

The concept of the perfect murder has long preoccupied not just crime writers, but also those who are determined to kill someone in real life. The secret of success usually lies in contriving the death so that it appears to be the result of natural causes, accident, or suicide. Crime writers have been guilty of concocting plots in which the only way the reader can be convinced of the culprit's direct involvement is for there to be a detailed confession—a tired fictional device. In reality, where there is a case of disguised murder, reliable forensic evidence is likely to be an indispensable tool in securing a conviction.

A simple form of murder disguised as accident occurs in cases of supposed falls, typically where a victim is lured to a cliff and pushed over the edge. This method is inherently unreliable, if only because the victim may survive the attack. It has been used countless times in fiction and is now seen as trite. Real life cases are much less common, but the ploy was utilized by Virginia McGinnis in California, in 1987 as a means of making a claim on a life insurance policy. She pushed Deana Wild to her death and claimed that the girl had slipped because she was wearing high heels. The jury, nevertheless, found McGinnis guilty of murder. In New Zealand, in 1954, two teenage girls, Pauline Parker and Juliet Hume, battered Parker's mother to death and pretended that the victim had slipped and fallen: a lie easily exposed by forensic evidence and compromising material in Parker's diary.

"Thinking murder" is therefore the best way for detectives to minimize the risk of a killer escaping justice. Death by hanging often occurs in suicide cases and sometimes happens by accident. It is relatively difficult for an unaided murderer to hang someone, but far from impossible. In 1925, Norman Thorne, an English chicken farmer, told police that he had found Elsie Cameron hanging from a rafter, but he was convicted for murder after his incompetence in staging her death was revealed: there were no rope marks on the beam and its top surface was coated with undisturbed dust. The death of Paula Gilfoyle in Merseyside, England, in 1992 was more difficult to interpret. She was found hanged in the family garage, and her husband Eddie showed police a suicide note that she had undoubtedly written. Further enquiries revealed a complex picture. Paula was pregnant, and it is extremely rare for pregnant women to kill themselves and their unborn babies. In addition, a reconstruction carried out by a pregnant police officer suggested that Paula could not have tied the rope to the beam herself. Eddie also claimed that he was studying suicide at the hospital where he worked, but this was untrue, and police decided that he had induced his wife to write the suicide note to assist him with his supposed studies and then killed her. Gilfoyle has always protested his innocence and an

unsuccessful attempt was made in 2001 to persuade the British appeal court to consider a psychological autopsy of Paula conducted by the eminent profiler David Canter that might have supported the notion that she killed herself.

Occasionally, "thinking murder" can be carried too far and result in a miscarriage of justice. In 1995, Ryan James, a British veterinary surgeon, was jailed for life and denounced by the judge as evil, selfish, and criminally callous. He was accused of killing his wife Sandra, who was found dead after drinking the drug Immobilon in a glass of orange juice. James had ready access to this drug through his work. His claim, that she had killed herself and staged the death as a murder in order to gain revenge for his infidelity, was rejected. But later, James's new wife found an apparent suicide note in the house and James was freed from prison. Police overlooked that fact that Sandra James would have had access to the Immobilon.

DETECTING THE MANNER OF DEATH

The criminologist Douglas Wynn has summarized the three key aspects of means to murder: availability, effectiveness, and detectability. In *The Crime Writer's Handbook* (1997) he goes so far as to offer gradings for a wide range of murder methods under those headings. The precise grades are, inevitably, debatable, but Wynn's broad classification is a useful analytical tool. In the Shipman case, the use of morphine was highly effective and difficult to detect until suspicion was aroused (not by a death in the series, but by a will that Shipman foolishly forged), but he was the only person to whom the fatal drug was available.

It is important not to forget the distinction between the cause of a death and the manner of it. The manner is, in effect, the cause of the cause of death: thus, a knife wound may cause the heart to stop, which in turn causes death. The focus in crime fiction is generally on the manner of death, but an accurate rendering of the procedure followed by forensic pathologists will also see the writer paying close attention to the direct cause.

ANIMALS, INSECTS, AND BACTERIA

From time to time, in both fiction and real life, murderers make use of animals, insects, or bacteria in committing their crimes. In the very first detective short story, *The Murders in the Rue Morgue* by Edgar Allan Poe (1841), the murders were shown by the amateur sleuth Dupin to have been accidental killings perpetrated by an orangutan. Sir Arthur Conan Doyle's *The Adventure of the Speckled Band* (1892) saw a swamp adder trained to kill. The case of Robert James of Los Angeles, who in 1936 failed to kill his wife with the aid of a rattlesnake before resorting to drowning her, illustrates the unreliability of members of the animal kingdom as tools of crime in real life. James had also bungled an attempt to kill his luckless victim with the aid of a poisonous spider. In 1992, Jeffrey Mann of Cleveland, Ohio, did succeed in tutoring a pit-bull to kill his girlfriend. He blamed the death on an attack by a strange dog. The flaw in his plan was that expert evidence showed the pit-bull to have been trained to attack, which it must have done repeatedly since the corpse was bitten 180 times. Mann was duly convicted.

Bacteria, in common with many poisons, are most readily available to medical workers and it is unsurprising that the few notable murder cases featuring bacterial poisoning include several doctors. In 1910, Dr. Bennett Clarke Hyde was accused of using a culture of typhoid germs to poison the heirs of a Kansas City millionaire. He was convicted, but there followed several appeals, a mistrial, and a failure on the part of the jury in the third trial to agree. The case against him was eventually dismissed. In 1916, a New York dentist named Arthur Warren Waite was found guilty of murdering his wife's parents. He implanted diphtheria and influenza germs into his mother-in-law's food, and for good measure gave his father-in-law a nasal spray loaded with tuberculosis bacteria. In 1969, a Houston, Texas, plastic surgeon named John Hill was suspected of killing his wife with a bacterial culture, but he was himself killed before he could stand trial.

BLUNT INSTRUMENTS

The blunt instrument is one of the least subtle of murder weapons. It is also one of the least effective. In the case of a single blow to the head, death is often more a matter of chance than judgment. Often, the blunt instrument is a means of committing murder on impulse, using the most readily available implement, and the killer frequently finds it necessary to resort to some other means, such as throat-cutting, to ensure the victim does not survive. Even when the crime is premeditated and the victim is outnumbered by the assailants, a blunt instrument may prove insufficient in itself, as the Snyder-Gray case of 1927 shows. Ruth Snyder and Henry Gray were

1 Pauline Parker (center) with classmates, eight months before she battered her mother to death in New Zealand in 1954.
2 Dr. Shipman's use of morphine was so subtle that even now the exact number of his victims is unknown.
3 The crude yet undeniably effective instruments used by the Yorkshire Ripper to murder his victims.
4 Rattlesnakes—a deadly but unreliable weapon.

FINGERPRINTING

Dr. Henry Faulds, a Scottish physiologist and medical missionary, is commonly regarded as the inventor of fingerprinting. He pioneered the use of "dactylography"—"finger-writing"—in solving crimes. In 1897, he was working in a hospital in Tokyo when a thief left a handprint on a wall at the scene of the crime. Faulds maintained that the suspect under arrest was not the culprit. Shortly afterwards, the real thief confessed and it was found that his handprint matched the one left at the scene.

At about the same time, an English clerk, William Herschel, conceived the theory that marks left by fingers do not change with age. Building on the work of Faulds and Herschel, the scientist Sir Francis Galton developed fingerprint identification into a science. He noted recurring shapes and configurations of lines in the infinite variety of fingerprints and recognized that in almost every print there was a triangle where the ridges ran together. Edward Henry, Inspector General of the Bengal Police, collaborated with Galton and listed the five main discernible patterns that would form the basis of a fingerprint identification system: arches, tented arches, radial loops, ulna loops, and whorls. The new system was adopted in the U.K. and in 1901 Henry took responsibility for a new Fingerprint Branch at police headquarters at Scotland Yard. Albert and Alfred Stratton, petty thieves who killed an old man in the course of committing a robbery, were convicted with the assistance of fingerprint evidence in 1905. By that time, fingerprint evidence had been used in jurisdictions as distant as Argentina. Henry's system was adopted by the FBI, and the first American killer to be convicted using fingerprint evidence was Thomas Jennings, who committed a murder in Chicago, in 1910. Soon, fingerprinting was helping to win the convictions of criminals, including murderers, all around the world.

Fingerprints can be made in several ways, often as invisible marks on surfaces or as impressions in soft substances such as soap. Visual prints may be photographed at the scene and then "lifted" by a transparent adhesive tape which can then be transferred to a card for recording and checking. Fingerprinting techniques have evolved to where palm print evidence is now also generally treated as acceptable evidence of identity. In major homicide cases, investigators may conduct mass fingerprinting or palm printing. Even where fingerprints are left on surfaces that in the past would not have lent themselves to effective fingerprinting, state of the art technology (an X-ray technique, for instance in the case of skin) may produce identification evidence. Latent prints can be revealed by dusting with powder or chemical reagents. Electrostatic methods and fluorescent techniques are sometimes employed—and so is superglue, which can produce good results in difficult cases. A number of fingerprint-classifying systems are in use around the world, but recent years have seen a move toward adopting 12-point standard matching prints.

A computer illustration of a fingerprint scan with colored markings showing the positions of characteristic features.

New York-based lovers who conspired to kill Snyder's husband. They both hit him with a heavy sash-weight, but had to use chloroform and picture wire to make sure he was dead. Snyder claimed the culprit was a prowler, but police were not deceived and the couple were both executed at Sing Sing prison.

Peter Sutcliffe, the Yorkshire Ripper, enjoyed much more success in eluding detection. He used a variety of household tools to kill thirteen women from 1975 to 1980, his principal weapon being a ball-peen hammer. When two police officers stopped him in connection with a minor offence, he tried quickly to hide his weapons, but their discovery by police helped to ensure his conviction.

BURNING

Murder by burning is rare. As a general rule, death is likely to occur when seventy percent of the skin is burned, although a much lower percentage of skin destruction may be fatal in some cases. Murderers more commonly use burning as a means to dispose of a corpse or at least to hide any evidence of murder. Sometimes burning is used to conceal the identity of the victim, but plans of this kind are frequently exposed, thanks to identification techniques practiced by forensic odontologists and others. A classic example is that of Alfred Arthur Rouse, a salesman from London, who, in 1930, murdered an unknown tramp by knocking him unconscious and setting fire to his own car with the dazed man inside it. Rouse confessed, shortly before his execution, confirming the interpretation of the crime scene put forward by a fire expert who had argued that the blaze was deliberately set rather than accidental. In Germany a year earlier, a Leipzig businessman

called Erich Tetzner murdered a hitchhiker, then burned the body in his car. The main difference between the two cases is that Tetzner's crime was essential to an insurance fraud. An unsolved case of burning involved a wealthy hotel owner, Sir Harry Oakes, in the Bahamas in 1943. The victim was beaten to death and the corpse partially burned. Theory has it that the culprits were members of the Mafia, who burned the corpse in ritual desecration to warn others against getting in their way.

DROWNING

Between 1912 and 1914, an Englishman, George Joseph Smith, made a career out of drowning his wives in the bath for financial gain. His MO was spotted only when the father of one of his victims read about the death of another in the newspaper. Smith's lawyer, the legendary Edward Marshall Hall, failed to persuade the judge to exclude evidence about the other deaths. Another celebrated figure in the case, the pathologist Bernard Spilsbury, gave evidence to the effect that the size of bath in which the last victim died precluded an accidental death. Spilsbury suggested that the murder in this case was committed by simultaneously lifting up the victim's knees and pushing down on her head.

Theodore Dreiser based his classic novel *An American Tragedy* (1925) on the case of Chester Gillette, an ambitious young man who in 1906

1 The burnt car belonging to Alfred Arthur Rouse, used to destroy the evidence of his crime.
2 George Joseph Smith and his first known victim, Bessie Mundy, from the Brides in the Bath case.
3 French woman Denise Labbe arrives at Blois courthouse escorted by Gendarmes. She is to be tried for the murder of her infant daughter.

took Billie Brown, a secretary whom he had made pregnant, for a boat trip on Big Moose Lake in New York State. Her body was washed up the following day. Gillette kept changing his story; at one time he said Billie had killed herself, at another he claimed she had drowned accidentally. This pointed to his guilt and he was sent to the electric chair.

People who are murdered by drowning are generally vulnerable in some way to their killers. In one particular French case, a woman, Denise Labbe, drowned her two-year-old daughter at the insistence of, and to prove her devotion to, her lover Jacques Algarron. Labbe saw her horrific act as a form of sacrifice. The couple were convicted in 1955.

A key issue in many cases of supposed death by drowning is whether the person was already dead when put into the water. The question can now be answered by diatom tests. Diatoms are tiny algae found in sea and fresh water. When someone drowns, water containing diatoms is sucked into the lungs. As the person struggles, the diatoms enter the bloodstream and are pumped around the body to the heart. An autopsy revealing the presence of diatoms proves that the victim was alive when he or she went into the water. It is possible for a corpse to have collected diatoms in its air passages, but they will not have been able to enter the bloodstream and travel to other organs.

EXPLOSIVES

A bomb or other explosive device may wreak havoc in a single incident. Timothy McVeigh killed 168 people, including many children, when he bombed the Alfred P. Murrah Federal Building in Oklahoma City, in 1995. The Unabomber, Ted Kaczynski, preferred to target individuals: using home-made bombs he waged a campaign of terror for sixteen years, targeting academics in particular, until the messages he sent to police finally yielded clues to his identity that led to his arrest and successful prosecution.

The hit-and-miss nature of explosions means that bombing is a risky technique for the murderer. In 1984, an English farmer, Graham Backhouse, planned to kill his wife in an explosion so that he could collect on her life insurance. He used a car bomb, supposedly targeted at himself, but his wife survived the incident and the clues that he had failed to clean up were sufficient to convict him of her attempted murder. In Florida the following year, in another attack motivated by greed, Steven Benson killed his mother and adopted brother, and injured his sister, in a car bomb attack. His unfeeling reaction to the tragedy, coupled with compelling forensic evidence—his palm print was found on receipts for parts of the bomb—helped to establish his guilt in the mind of investigators and, ultimately, the court.

FIREARMS

Firearms (other than crossbows, which are occasionally used as murder weapons) fall into two categories: smooth-bore or rifled. The inside of the barrel is smooth in the former, rough in the latter. In larger smooth-bore weapons, the diameter of the inside of the barrel, usually known as the caliber or gauge, is sized in an old-fashioned way by

1 The weapons of John Dillinger. The machine gun, bulletproof vest, and automatic were the stock in trade of this gangster during his career.
2 The Unabomber pictured at the start of his trial in Sacramento, California.
3 Jacques Mesrine, pictured after he was shot dead by officers following a lengthy chase.

reference to the number of lead balls that fit exactly inside the barrel and which weigh one pound. If it takes twelve lead balls to weigh one pound, for instance, the weapon is called a 12-gauge. Smooth-bore guns are mostly shotguns, mainly designed for sport shooting, and may have either one or two barrels. In a double-barreled gun, one barrel is usually choked (choking holds the shot together over long distances) while the other is a cylinder barrel. The gun may be a single-shot weapon that breaks beyond the stock so that the barrel drops down and the fired cartridges can be taken out and the gun reloaded by hand. Slide or pump-action shotguns have a slide below the barrel that, when moved, automatically puts another cartridge in the firing chamber and closes the breech; the cartridge is usually ejected after firing. Sawn-off shotguns, frequently used in armed robberies, have the barrel(s) and stock cut to make it easier to hide them, although this limits their uses since the shot spreads too quickly to permit penetration at long distance.

Rifled handguns may be either pistols or revolvers. Revolvers have a cylindrical magazine with five or six chambers, each holding a cartridge. Cocking the hammer of a single-action revolver with the thumb brings the next chamber into firing position. Double-action revolvers may be cocked by applying pressure to the trigger. Pistols have a sealed chamber in the barrel and a hollow butt into which the magazine fits. They are often called automatics, but a more accurate term is semi-automatic or self-loading. The spent cartridge is ejected automatically. Single-shot automatics have to be loaded manually each time the gun is fired. Modern cartridges are metal cylinders designed to fit the gun-chamber. In the center of the base of the cylinder, a soft metal cap

contains a primer charge that is crushed when the gun's firing pin sets off the main propellant. The primer and the propellant leave telltale traces of dust and powder on close-range targets and the hand of the shooter.

FIREARMS CASES

Rifles are fired from the shoulder and are used, typically by snipers and assassins, for long-distance shooting. Some are described as automatics, although again they are only true automatics if they keep firing as long as the trigger is pressed. Machine and sub-machine guns, similarly, may be either automatics or semi-automatics. They fire pistol ammunition but generally need to be held in both hands. The nature of wounds made by a rifled firearm depends on the type of gun. With a handgun, the entry wound is usually a small round or oval hole surrounded by inflamed skin. The exit wound (if there is one) will be larger and irregular in shape. Extensive bleeding is unusual. A rifle bullet may cause a larger wound, with some designed to cause extensive damage to body tissue.

The barrels of rifled firearms have spiral grooves cut on the inside. The purpose of the grooves is to improve accuracy in firing, but the grooves leave marks on the bullet and no two barrels leave quite the same striations. This feature helps ballistics experts to identify firearms used to commit murders and plays an important part in homicide detection.

Firearms feature in countless homicides, ranging from straightforward domestic murders to political killings (both John F. Kennedy and Martin Luther King, Jr., were killed with rifles) and mass murders. One of the most dramatic family crimes occurred in England, in 1985, when five members of Jeremy Bamber's family were killed with a .22 Anschutz semi-automatic rifle. It seemed that Bamber's ill, troubled sister Sheila Caffell had killed the others and then shot herself. But with a silencer attached, the weapon would measure forty-nine inches and to have reached the trigger and shot herself through the chin, Sheila would have needed very long arms. The police concluded that Bamber had staged the crimes for financial gain, and the jury agreed.

One of the most unsatisfactory murder cases in American history concerned two anarchists, Nicola Sacco and Bartolomeo Vanzetti, who were tried in 1921 for a double killing committed in the course of a payroll robbery. The case against them rested on unsatisfactory evidence that the murder weapon was Sacco's .32 Colt pistol. During a protracted series of appeals, a firearms expert called Calvin Goddard sought to demonstrate, with the aid of a comparison microscope (that enables the marks on a crime bullet and a test bullet to be matched microscopically in a single image) that Sacco's gun was indeed the murder weapon. The two men were duly sent to the electric chair but substantial doubts persist, especially about Vanzetti's guilt.

For a period of twelve months beginning in July 1976, a killer known as Son of Sam terrorized New York using a .44 Bulldog revolver to murder six people and seriously wound seven others. After one of the crimes, the culprit, David Berkowitz, encountered a police checkpoint. His gun lay loaded and in full view on the passenger seat of his car, but the checkpoint was ended before Berkowitz reached the front of the line. Spree killers like Berkowitz almost always use firearms. In 1949, Howard Unruh of New Jersey killed thirteen people in as many minutes with a Luger pistol. In August 1987, the English gun fanatic Michael

Ryan murdered sixteen people and wounded fourteen more before turning his Kalashnikov AK-47 upon himself. Nine years later Martin Bryant became Australia's most prolific spree killer using an AR-15 semi-automatic rifle. In 2001 Friedrich Leibacher vented a petty grievance by running amok in the Swiss regional parliament building at Zug near Zurich, killing fifteen with an arsenal of weapons including an assault rifle, a pump-action shotgun, a pistol, and a revolver.

Firearms are used by criminals to perpetrate a crime, such as theft, and murder is sometimes incidental to their activities. In 1952, two young Englishmen named Christopher Craig and Derek Bentley were carrying out a burglary when the police arrived. Craig pulled out a revolver and Bentley shouted "Let him have it." Craig fatally wounded one policeman, but was too young to hang. Despite the ambiguity of his words, which might have been a message to surrender the gun rather than to fire, Bentley was executed. In contrast, John Dillinger, a robber who acquired an almost mythical reputation for shooting his way out of trouble in 1930s America, was eventually himself gunned down by the FBI. The precise circumstances of his death have been much debated and rumors persist that the dead man was in fact only impersonating Dillinger, who supposedly escaped justice and lived to a ripe old age in Hollywood under an assumed name.

KNIVES AND OTHER SHARP IMPLEMENTS

The most famous serial killer of all, Jack the Ripper, used a knife to commit his crimes in nineteenth century Whitechapel, London, and knives remain popular and formidable weapons in the hands of those with murderous inclinations.

They were used by Juan Vallejo Corona, a Mexican labor contractor who was convicted on twenty five counts of murder in the Californian Superior Court in 1971. Other throat-cutting serial killers include German factory worker Peter Kurten, the Monster of Dusseldorf, and Ed Kemper, the Co-ed Killer, a necrophiliac who terrorized Santa Cruz County in California in the early 1970s.

Stab wounds are characterized by their penetration into the body. Because the entry points may appear insignificant, with little bleeding, the seriousness of a knife wound can easily be underestimated. The delay that sometimes occurs between the inflicting of a knife wound and the victim's collapse and death has sometimes been utilized by authors for plot purposes: an example is to be found in Agatha Christie's *Ordeal by Innocence* (1958). In the Wigwam case of 1942, a French-Canadian soldier stationed in Britain, August Sangret, stabbed and bludgeoned to death a young woman who had taken to living outdoors (hence the Wigwam title) and buried her body in a shallow grave. After it was uncovered, the pathologist Keith Simpson discovered that the stab wounds had been inflicted with an unusual knife that had a hook-like point resembling a parrot's beak. The weapon was successfully traced to Sangret, and helped to establish his guilt.

POISON

Poisoning is an age-old murder method, the popularity of which has declined over the past one hundred and fifty years as a result of the increasing sophistication of toxicological detective work. Traditionally, the appeal of poison to the murderer was that its symptoms often resemble those of ordinary ailments, making the very existence of a crime hard to prove. Arsenic poisoning, for example, produces symptoms similar to those of gastro-enteritis. Furthermore, many lethal poisons are often easy to obtain, despite the strengthening of legal controls in many jurisdictions; poisons are often available over the counter for household, veterinary, or garden use. Even drugs whose use is strictly regulated may be readily available to doctors, nurses, dentists, or veterinarians, and it is noteworthy that in many famous poisoning cases the culprit has been a medical worker.

An added attraction of poison is the many ways in which it can be administered, typically disguised in food, drink, or medicine. Poison may be ingested, inhaled, absorbed, or injected. Although "undetectable" poisons, favored by many crime writers of the past, seem a tired cliché nowadays, complications of analysis continue to arise in cases where the poison breaks down into constituent elements already present in the human body. An example is succinylcholine chloride, which splits into the succinic acid and choline that a pathologist would expect to discover in human body tissue. Even here, however, it is possible to detect a homicide. In 1984, Texas nurse Genene Jones was convicted of murdering a fifteen-month-old child in her care, Chelsea McClellan, by administering succinylcholine. The evidence against her appeared to be thin, but gas liquid chromatography, used to analyze the tissues of Chelsea's exhumed body once suspicion was aroused, showed traces of succinylcholine.

Victims of a mass cult poisoning in the United States. The poison was self-administered.

Various attempts have been made to classify poisons. Perhaps the most widely accepted is to divide them into four broad categories. One group includes acids and alkalis that have a corrosive effect. If swallowed, they burn the mouth and cause the stomach to perforate. They may also be used in an attempt to dispose of an inconvenient body.

A second category is substances that affect the oxygen-carrying capacity of the blood, causing rapid respiratory failure followed by death. Examples are carbon monoxide and cyanide. The former is an odorless gas, and the hemoglobin of human blood has such an affinity for it that it will absorb it three hundred times faster than oxygen. As the body is insidiously saturated with carbon monoxide and starved of oxygen, it suffers asphyxiation. Cyanide, on the other hand, comes in various forms, including hydrocyanic acid (also called prussic acid). Cyanide is seldom a weapon of mass murderers but in the Jonestown Massacre in Guyana, in 1979, cult members died by drinking or being forced to drink it.

The third group contains the systemic poisons that are absorbed by the body, damaging the liver, kidneys, and nervous and circulatory systems. Arsenic was, for many years, the murderer's poison of choice, until improvements in toxicological analysis made its use increasingly risky. The human body can build up a tolerance to arsenic, a fact that Dorothy L. Sayers exploited skilfully in *Strong Poison* (1930). Queen Elizabeth I of England is said to have used arsenic as a cosmetic, and in the nineteenth century peasants in the Austrian province of Styria took small doses of arsenic with their food because they thought it conducive to both health and beauty. Similarly, James Maybrick, who died in Liverpool, England, was reputed to take arsenic because of its supposed aphrodisiac properties. When he died in 1889 following a short illness, suspicion in the troubled Maybrick household at Battlecrease House focused on Maybrick's American wife, Florence. She had—like her husband—been engaging in an affair. She had also purchased flypaper containing arsenic from a local pharmacist. After a hostile summing-up from a judge who shortly afterward succumbed to mental illness, she was found guilty of murdering Maybrick. Following a campaign by sympathizers on both sides of the Atlantic her death sentence was commuted to life imprisonment, and after spending fifteen years in jail she was eventually released. It remains unclear whether she was responsible for her husband's death and Anthony Berkeley's novel based on the Maybrick story, *The Wychford Poisoning Case* (1926), details a number of possible solutions to the mystery. In a bizarre footnote to the Maybrick case, 1991 saw the publication of a diary, allegedly written by James and identifying him as Jack the Ripper. Intensive scientific analysis has failed to establish conclusively whether the diary is a fake or not. If it is a work of fiction, its unknown author's ingenuity was great indeed.

Other poisons falling in to this category include antimony, mercury, and plant poisons or vegetable alkaloids such as strychnine, morphine, and hyoscin. Dr. Thomas Neill Cream practiced as

1 A Jack the Ripper feature suggesting that James Maybrick was in fact the Ripper and author of recently found diaries supposedly written by the as yet unidentified murderer.
2 High-pressure liquid chromatography equipment being used to identify poisons in a forensic laboratory.

Is this the face of Jack the Ripper?

by Colin Adamson

THE final piece of a jigsaw which has baffled criminologists for 105 years was slotted into place today when Victorian cotton broker James Maybrick was named as Jack the Ripper.

Maybrick, a bizarre character who took arsenic to boost his sex life and was later murdered by his wife with a dose of the same poison, is accused of the notorious Whitechapel murders in a forthcoming book.

Publishers Smyth Gryphon, who had hoped to keep their new findings under wraps until publication in October, claim their case is solidly based on what they say is a fully authenticated 62-page diary kept by the Liverpool businessman.

But today, the Liverpool Daily Post blew the closely-guarded secret.

Paul Begg, co-author of The A to Z of Jack the Ripper, told the newspaper that everyone who had seen the diary had signed a confidentiality agreement.

He says: "The diary is signed, the signature is Jack the Ripper."

Maybrick died in 1889, the year after the Ripper killings. He was a womaniser and a drug addict with a reputation for violent behaviour, a morose disposition and a fierce temper.

He was said to be a notorious frequenter of brothels on his travels to cotton ports around the world and once admitted to a New York specialist in nervous diseases that he was a "victim of free-living, alcohol abuse and other excesses".

His wife Florence, 20 years his younger, finally snapped and killed him. She had her death sentence commuted to life imprisonment and died penniless and in squalor in America in 1941.

Maybrick's brother Michael was said to be an amateur composer who composed songs and sea shanties, including one little ditty called They All Love Jack.

Although experts are becoming increasingly convinced that the diary is not going to turn into a fiasco like Hitler's Diaries, there was always one potential hole in the argument.

No one had proved what antique dealers call provenance — where the diary had been since 1888.

But Paul Feldman, of MIA Production, who made a TV film to coincide with the book, revealed in Monday's Evening Standard that he had final proof.

"It was hidden in the man's home and came to light when something was touched that had not been touched for 105 years," he said.

If the new book does, in fact, point the finger directly at Maybrick, it will be the first time he has been linked with the Ripper murders.

So far, the vast army of Ripperologists has thrown up no fewer than 72 suspects, from Lord Randolph Churchill and the Duke of Clarence to Queen Victoria's doctor, Sir William Gull.

The diary is said to have been written by "a husband and father from north of Watford."

Among the more comprehensible passages is: "I will take the first whore I encounter and show what hell is really like.

"All the bitches will pay for the pain. Before I am finished, all England will know the name I have given myself."

Florence Maybrick: Murdered her husband, now thought to have been the Ripper

James Maybrick: Accused of the murders

the face of
e Ripper?

a physician in Chicago until 1881 when he was convicted of the murder of his mistress's husband, whom he poisoned with strychnine. On his release, ten years later, he moved to London and started giving prostitutes pills containing strychnine. He claimed four victims before his obsessive need to draw attention to himself led to his arrest and eventual execution.

The fourth group of poisons includes those that leave no trace of entry. The classic example is ricin, which achieved lasting fame through a single unsolved murder case. In 1978, Georgi Markov, a Bulgarian defector living in London was in line for a bus when he felt a stab of pain in his thigh. He noticed a man picking up an umbrella as he hailed a cab. Markov's leg felt sore, but he did not consult a doctor until the next day. Three days later Markov was dead and laboratory tests revealed a tiny pellet embedded in his leg. Its cavities had contained one-fifth of a milligram of a toxin, presumed to be ricin, a derivative of castor oil bean husks. Based on what Markov saw, the widely held view is that an umbrella-gun was used to fire the pellet containing ricin into his leg. The killer was never brought to justice, but the Bulgarian secret service was inevitably implicated.

Traditionally, poisonings in crime fiction have occurred in relatively genteel circumstances, perhaps because the poisoner has been perceived as a solitary figure, often working in a domestic environment. In recent years, the activities of the Aum cult, which originated in Japan, and the threat of global terrorism have highlighted the potential of nerve agents such as sarin, which was used by the Aum cult, for inflicting large-scale casualties. A single 500-pound bomb made from sarin could wipe out half the population of a major city.

STRANGULATION

Strangulation causes death by asphyxia. It can be done either by hand—in which case the killing cannot be confused with accident or suicide—or with the aid of a cord, usually called a garotte or ligature. Manual strangulation, or throttling, is generally inflicted by a stronger person on a weaker one. An effective ligature may be formed, for example, from a rope, tie, scarf, or belt. Law enforcement officers investigating the crime need to photograph the knot on the ligature before it is removed, since it may provide pointers to the offender. Usually, strangulation is accompanied by sexual assault.

Albert DeSalvo, the Boston Strangler, established his MO with his first murder, the killing of Anna Slesers. The cord of her housecoat was tightly knotted around her neck and tied into a clumsily bow. Thereafter, details of his crimes varied: in the second case, the victim was strangled with two of her own nylon stockings; and in the third a nylon stocking was used with a bra looped through and the straps knotted beneath the chin. DeSalvo's basic method remained the same, however, giving clues to his identity.

The fallibility of expert evidence is shown by the English case of Harold Loughans, accused in 1943 of the manual strangulation of Rose Robinson. Forensic evidence linked him with the crime, but the defence lawyers called the eminent pathologist Sir Bernard Spilsbury who testified that Loughans could not have committed the crime. This was on account of Loughans' deformed right hand. The prosecution relied on the view of another noted pathologist, Keith Simpson, that the disability was no impediment to murder, but Loughans was acquitted. When he was dying seventeen years later, Loughans admitted his guilt.

SUFFOCATION AND SMOTHERING

Suffocation and smothering cause death by asphyxiation. The obstruction of a victim's nose and mouth stop the breathing process, and within half a minute the victim may be rendered unconscious, with death following soon afterward. Typically, victims are vulnerable, whether through old age, youth, or intoxication.

In an English case in 1948, a burglar named George Russell was convicted of suffocating ninety-year-old Mrs Freeman Lee. He battered her head, tied her up, and put her in a trunk where, deprived of oxygen, she died. Victims at the other end of the age scale include three babies of Marybeth Tinning's of Schenectady, New York. She put pillows over their faces, and at first, doctors believed that the children had died of natural causes. In 1991, Beverley Allitt (see below), the English nurse who committed a series of murders and assaults on children under her care, used a variety of methods including asphyxiation.

Albert DeSalvo, the Boston Strangler, who says he strangled thirteen women, is held by police officers moments after his capture in Lynn, Massachusetts. He is still wearing the navy uniform from the mental hospital from which he escaped.

OKLAHOMA BOMBING

On April 19, 1995, a bomb destroyed the Alfred P. Murrah Federal Building in Oklahoma City, killing 168 people and injuring more than five hundred. The initial assumption made by law enforcement agencies was that a foreign terrorist group was responsible. However, the attack occurred on the second anniversary of the conclusion of the siege of the Branch Davidian compound at Waco, Texas.

The FBI recovered the vehicle identification number of the truck used to deliver the bomb and traced the location from which it had been rented. A description of the renter was turned into a sketch by FBI artists. A motel owner recognized the face and gave investigators the name of Timothy McVeigh, adding that he had been surprised by the vehemence of McVeigh's reaction to the Waco shoot-out. In the meantime, McVeigh had been arrested for a traffic offense and for carrying a concealed firearm, and was already in prison when FBI agents came to interview him about the bombings. When his clothes were tested, residue from the detonation cord was detected on his shirt.

It turned out that Waco was a kind of trigger for McVeigh. He used it as an excuse to vent his anger and frustration at a society in which he had failed to succeed, as a reason why he could commit acts of violence without—in his own mind—being responsible for them. He had spent three years in the army, but was unable to achieve his goal of joining the Special Forces. After taking a job as a security guard, he started writing to newspapers complaining about various types of government corruption. His preferred reading was books that were racist and anti-establishment. He had traveled to Waco during consensus standoff between government forces and cult members, selling bumper stickers with slogans such as "Fear the Government That Fears Your Guns." After his arrest he described himself as a prisoner of war: a sign of his refusal to accept personal accountability for the carnage he had caused. The forensic evidence linking McVeigh to the crime withstood critical scrutiny in court and the bomber was sentenced to death. He was executed by lethal injection in 2001.

The profiler John Douglas has highlighted the range of possible motivations of a bomber. He may be seeking political power, carrying out what he regards as a mission, or simply taking revenge against a society that he believes has let him down. As Douglas points out, McVeigh matched key profiling assumptions in a bombing case: he was a white male, an under-achiever with the ability to plan meticulously, and a cowardly, inadequate loner. Suggestions that McVeigh was the tool of a sophisticated conspiracy have never been proven, although he was assisted by an equally inadequate accomplice, Terry Nichols, who was given a life sentence.

1 The damage done to the Alfred P. Murrah Federal Building after the bombing is all too clear.
2 Rescue workers check the rubble for clues as to the type of bomb used and any evidence that might lead to the maker of the bomb itself.
3 Timothy McVeigh at the federal penitentiary.

TOTALLY RATTLED

The unreliability of reptiles and insects as murder weapons is illustrated by the comedy of errors experienced by Robert James in the course of his attempts to kill his pregnant wife Mary in 1935. James, a Los Angeles barber, had been married five times in all; one of his previous wives had drowned in her bath and, although suspicion was not aroused at the time, it seems likely that he was responsible for that death and perhaps others. There was an insurance policy on Mary and James was anxious to profit from it, but wanted to try a method of murder that would appear to be an accident.

When a handyman named Charles Hope told James he was broke and asked for a haircut on credit, the barber sensed an opportunity. He offered Hope the chance to earn some money if he knew anything about rattlesnakes because he had a "friend" whose wife was bothering him and who wanted to have a snake bite her. Hope duly supplied James with a snake that had come from a local sideshow. James decided to test the snake's killing potential by putting it into a box full of chickens. The chickens seemed unruffled, so James and Hope bought another snake, from another sideshow, and put it into a box with a rabbit. The following morning James found the snake dead but the rabbit alive and well. Hope then supplied James with two Crotalus atrox rattlesnakes that had come straight from the Colorado desert. When these killed the chickens, James, who had by now taken Hope into his confidence, sought the other man's help in using the snakes to kill Mary.

Mary, in the meantime, had agreed to have an abortion and James told his wife that the illegal operation would be carried out by Hope. In order that she could not testify against Hope if the authorities ever investigated, she would have to be blindfolded during the abortion. Further, she would have to be strapped on the kitchen table and have her lips sealed with adhesive tapes. Mary unwisely agreed and her foot was then thrust into the box containing the rattlesnakes, which bit her. Hope then left to sell the snakes back to the supplier. But although Mary was by now in much pain, she did not die. Frustrated, James reverted to his previous MO and drowned her in the bath. With Hope's help, he then put the body in a lily pond in his garden.

Despite the almost comic incompetence of the criminals, Mary's death was treated as a suicide until, months later and following receipt of information in an anonymous letter, the authorities learned that James had been having sexual relations with his niece. Mary's corpse was exhumed and traces of rattlesnake venom discovered. Hope admitted his involvement and earned a life sentence. James was executed.

Rattlesnakes are not the most reliable killing weapon, although their deadly venom can cause death in the end if the victim is not treated.

THE YORKSHIRE RIPPER

On a cold October morning in 1975, a milkman in Leeds, England, discovered a woman's body. It was found to be Wilma McCann, a prostitute. Her chest and stomach were lacerated with fourteen stab wounds and a post mortem revealed that she had been attacked from behind and hit hard twice on the back of the head with a hammerlike implement. One blow had shattered her skull; the stabbings had taken place after death. There was no obvious sexual motive and the victim's purse was missing so the police treated the crime as murder in the course of robbery.

Less than three months later an occasional prostitute called Emily Jackson was found dead in Leeds. There were similarities with the McCann killing, but Emily's body had been stabbed over fifty times, her back being gouged with a screwdriver. More murders occurred and, though it has been suggested that at first the investigation dawdled because the murdered women were prostitutes, soon the exploits of the so-called Yorkshire Ripper were causing panic throughout the North of England, and a massive manhunt was launched. Several of his victims,

such as shop assistant Jayne MacDonald and clerk Josephine Whittaker, were not prostitutes, so it was clear that no woman was safe until the Ripper was caught. The police investigation was riddled with flaws and precious resources were devoted to trying to trace the sender of a tape, supposedly from the Yorkshire Ripper, which proved to be a hoax.

After the Ripper had killed thirteen times, the detectives had a stroke of luck. They saw a man soliciting a prostitute in Sheffield and decided to question him. His license plates were false and

he was taken in for questioning. When officers returned to the place where they had apprehended him, they discovered a ball-peen hammer and a knife. The man, a truck driver and former gravedigger named Peter Sutcliffe, quickly admitted that he was the Yorkshire Ripper. He pleaded not guilty to thirteen murders and seven attempted murders by reason of diminished responsibility: defense psychiatrists diagnosed him as a paranoid schizophrenic who claimed to have been acting on the instructions of God. The prosecution contended that his story of a divine mission to kill was a fabrication designed to lessen his punishment. When the jury found him guilty, the judge sentenced him to life imprisonment and recommended that he serve at least thirty years.

Sutcliffe used household tools as his weapons. At his trial, more than thirty implements were produced in court, including seven ball-peen hammers, a claw hammer, and a hacksaw. There was also a cobbler's knife and a piece of rope that Sutcliffe had intended to use to strangle some of his victims. He tried to cut off the head of one victim, Jean Jordan, thinking this would conceal his telltale hammer blow signature.

1 Detectives discover yet another victim of the Yorkshire Ripper and execute a thorough search of the surrounding area.
2 Peter Sutcliffe is taken to the magistrate's court.

GAS ATTACK

Shoko Asahara, whose real name was Chizuo Matsumoto, was born partially blind in 1955, but determined that disability would not prevent him from becoming rich. He began by establishing an acupuncture clinic that offered remedies of dubious value and indulged in a variety of frauds. After developing an interest in meditation, he soon realized the intense appeal of fantasy and fundamentalism in religious cults. So, in 1984 he created a company called Aum Inc. (Aum is a Hindu mantra said to incorporate the truth of the universe.)

Within a couple of years he had acquired the name Asahara, a dense beard, and the ivory-white attire expected of a holy man. Aum Supreme Truth became a highly effective money-making machine, a cult attracting thousands of young adherents who responded to its bizarre but exciting promises of enlightenment, community, and supernatural power.

Cult members who expressed doubts about Aum were killed by fanatical followers. As Aum's wealth grew, Asahara had the power to despatch hit squads to silence his enemies, but before long he tired of individual slayings and turned his attention to Armageddon.

Aum scientists researched various weapons of mass destruction and the cult spent over ten million U.S. dollars establishing a factory to produce nerve gas. Its weapon of choice was isopropyl methylphosphonofluoridate, better known as sarin, which is relatively easy to produce from widely available raw materials. A single drop of this odorless and colorless nerve agent is enough to kill.

Although the Japanese authorities had at first been slow to respond to the threat posed by Aum, the Tokyo police were, by 1995, pursuing their investigations into the cult's activities with more vigor. Aum decided to deal a crippling blow to the investigation by targeting Tokyo's vast subway system: two attackers would release sarin on each of three main subway lines. The city would be paralyzed and Aum would have embarked on its historic mission of world domination.

The attacks were launched on March 20, 1995 and caused pandemonium. Over five and a half thousand people were affected by the nerve gas, many of them suffering serious injuries. There were twelve deaths. The toll would have been much worse but for impurities in the sarin. Aum was an obvious suspect and one thousand officers in riot gear and chemical warfare suits raided the cult's Mount Fuji stronghold, where they uncovered a massive stockpile of weapons. Japan was gripped by panic as Asahara and his disciples made thinly veiled threats of reprisals, and calm was not restored until the guru was finally arrested on May 16, 1995. The cult subsequently began to fall apart, but not before it had given the world a frightening glimpse of the potential for high-tech terrorism, and the dangers that face civilization if governments and law enforcement agencies fail to deal swiftly and effectively with fanatics who have access to weapons of mass destruction.

A member of the Aum cult is arrested for holding cult members illegally in the Yamanashi raid.

BODY IN THE CELLAR

When Belle Elmore, a vivacious but unsuccessful music hall artiste, suddenly disappeared in 1910, her friends were puzzled. Her husband, an amiable Michigan-born homeopathic physician named Crippen, who had settled with her in London a few years earlier, assured police that Belle had needed to return to the U.S. to handle urgent family business. As Belle's concerned friends pressed for more information, he told them that he had been informed that his wife had died of pneumonia, and he placed an obituary in a theatrical newspaper. Belle's friends became suspicious when Crippen installed his secretary, Ethel Le Neve, in his household and she began wearing items of Belle's jewelry. Scotland Yard was informed and Crippen readily admitted to Chief Inspector Walter Dew that he had lied about his wife who, he now claimed, had simply deserted him, presumably to join her lover in the U.S.

2

The initial police inquiries made little headway until Crippen and Le Neve bolted to continental Europe. The Crippen home at 39 Hilldrop Crescent, Camden Town, London, was searched thoroughly and human remains were found buried in the cellar. A large-scale hunt for Crippen and his lover ensued and they were found, disguised as a father and son named Robinson, by the captain of the Canadian-bound ship aboard which the couple hoped to make their escape. When the ship landed at Quebec, Dew was waiting to arrest them.

Crippen's trial became the stuff of legend. Bernard Spilsbury, a pathologist previously unknown to the public, made his reputation by identifying the remains, thanks to a distinguishing scar, as those of Belle Elmore, but the evidence of Dr. William Willcox, a Home Office scientific advisor, was at least as significant. Willcox explained that the deceased had been poisoned with hydrobromide of hyoscin, an alkaloid found in plants such as henbane. Crippen had purchased the drug a few months before his wife's death but claimed to have bought it for his patients. He was a purveyor of quack remedies and said that his blood and nerve tonic for obstinate cases of nerve diseases and spasmodic ailments contained hyoscin. His calm and dignified manner in the witness box won him some sympathy, but the prosecutor's cross-examination was devastating. The jury took only twenty-seven minutes to find the meek little doctor guilty of Belle's murder. Crippen was hanged, but Ethel was acquitted; the consensus was that she knew nothing of Belle's fate.

Although Crippen disputed it, there can be little or no doubt that the remains found in the cellar belonged to Belle and that, making use of his anatomical knowledge, he had ruthlessly dismembered her corpse before trying unsuccessfully to destroy it with quicklime. What is less clear is how she came to be poisoned. One theory holds that Crippen intended to use the drug as a sedative or as a means of depressing her voracious sexual appetite, but that through characteristic incompetence he accidentally administered a fatal overdose.

1 A newspaper report describes the story of Dr. Crippen's murder case and eventual capture.
2 Dr. Crippen in the dock with Ethel Le Neve at the start of their trial for murder.

CONTRACT KILLING

The dangers of relying on contract killers are illustrated by the case of Christine and Peter Demeter. Christine, a glamorous Austrian-born blonde, was found dead on the garage floor of her home in Toronto, Canada, in July 1973. Her head was smashed in, although the murder weapon was never found. The body was found by her husband, a real-estate developer.

Peter Demeter had a cast-iron alibi for the killing but his boorish behavior and apparent lack of grief soon antagonized investigators. Soon, the family's maid revealed to detectives that Demeter was involved with another woman, Marina Hundt, who was just as attractive as his wife. Demeter admitted that his marriage had been troubled and the maid confirmed that she had witnessed various quarrels. Further, he had recently taken out a million-dollar (U.S.) insurance policy on Christine's life. A family friend, Csaba Szilagyi, described how he and Demeter had discussed various ways of killing Christine. The police bugged a conversation between Szilagyi and Demeter, in which Demeter urged his friend to refuse to take a lie-detector test. Demeter did not make an outright confession, but what he said could be interpreted as indicating guilt.

Demeter was arrested and charged with Christine's murder, and a prosecution witness, Freddie Stark, testified that he had arranged a contract killer for Demeter, by the name of Cutlip Kacsa. Kacsa was supposed to push Christine down the stairs, but lost his nerve at the last minute. Unfortunately Kacsa had left Canada for Hungary and died before he could be extradited. Szilagyi's testimony fared badly under cross-examination and the taped conversation with Demeter, although allowed as evidence, was far from conclusive. The case then took a wholly unexpected turn: two weeks before Demeter's trial, an escaped convict called Laszlo Eper had been killed in a shootout with police. In his room was a piece of paper bearing Demeter's name. An associate of Eper's, Joe Dinardo, claimed that Eper had approached him on behalf of Christine Demeter, who wanted her husband dead. Dinardo said he had not wanted to become involved, but later Eper had come to him in a panic: his clothes were covered in blood and he claimed that after an argument over money, he had killed Christine. The prosecutor argued that Dinardo's evidence was inadmissible since it was hearsay, and the judge agreed. As a result, the jury never heard from Dinardo. They did not have to decide who actually killed Christine, merely whether Demeter was responsible for his wife's murder. After considering the evidence for only three hours, they brought in a guilty verdict and Demeter was sentenced to life in prison.

Peter Demeter is led to jail after his conviction for the murder of his wife Christine.

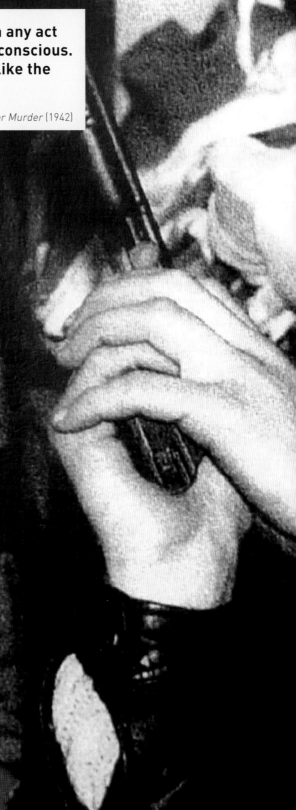

> **"No human being can ever perform any act without a motive, conscious or unconscious. The unmotivated act was a myth, like the unicorn or a sea serpent."**
>
> Helen McCloy, *Cue for Murder* (1942)

To prove the guilt of a murderer in court, prosecutors need to produce compelling evidence. Murder investigations are structured with a view to obtaining such evidence. However, to win a conviction prosecutors do not need to prove why the murderer committed the crime. Attempts to penetrate the thought processes of a murder suspect are often fraught with difficulty, especially if the suspect is uncooperative and refuses to answer questions, either during the investigation or in court.

This does not mean that investigators can ignore the motive for the crime or that it is futile to attempt to determine it. The eminent profiler John Douglas maintains in *The Anatomy of Motive* (1999, with Mark Olshaker) that there is no such thing as a motiveless crime, that "every crime has a motive." The precise truth about the killer's motivation may never be clear, but murder investigators have become aware of the importance of trying to work out what may have gone on inside the head of an unknown killer.

There are good reasons why the analysis of motive is crucial in many murder investigations.

A photograph found in the apartment of Barry George who was convicted of killing Jill Dando.

Previous page: Subway passengers lie on the ground after being evacuated from Tokyo Underground, following the sarin attack in 1995.

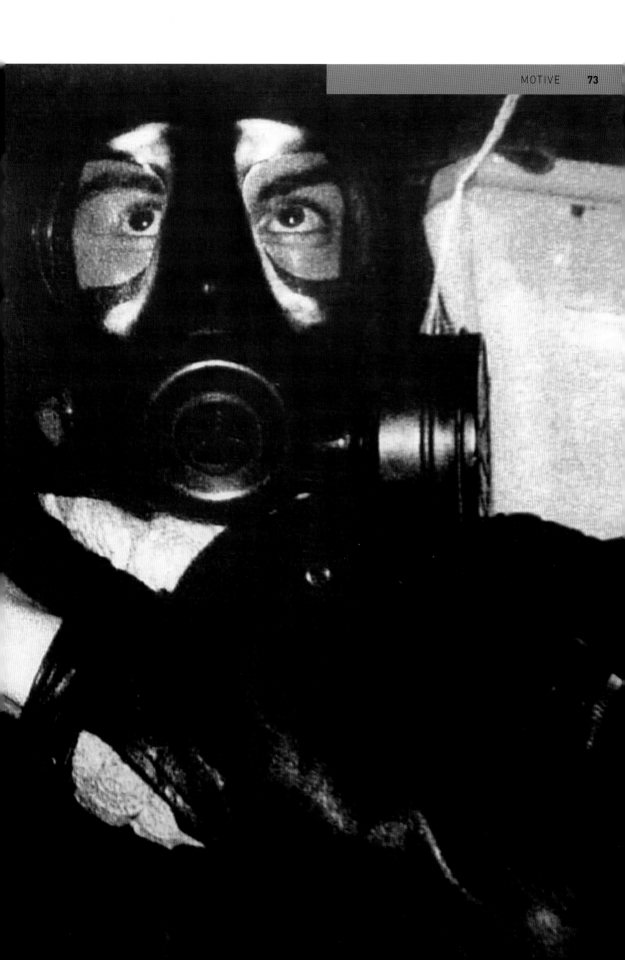

At the end of a trial, a jury that is unclear about why the accused may have killed the victim is less likely to conclude that the accused is guilty beyond a reasonable doubt. Long before the case comes to court, failure to understand the reason for the crime will hamper the investigation and may even fail to produce a credible suspect. Time and valuable resources may be wasted if investigators do not focus quickly on the correct line of questioning. Delay is the enemy of a successful investigation. As time passes, evidence and witnesses may disappear and the chances of bringing the killer to justice decline.

An important lesson for crime writers and enthusiasts is that the motive must be credible and interesting. This means understanding not only the victim but also his or her killer. If the reason why the crime was committed does not seem adequate or believable, a book is likely to fail just as would a prosecution.

WHY KILL JILL DANDO?

Few cases better illustrate the truth that understanding motive is at the heart of a murder investigation than the 1999 shooting of the BBC television personality Jill Dando. She was killed outside her front door in London one morning, by a single 9mm bullet. No one in the area witnessed the crime. One of the largest and most high-profile murder hunts in the history of British law enforcement followed, conducted throughout in a blaze of publicity. The brutal, and seemingly very professional, killing of a much-loved media personality put the investigators under intense pressure to bring the culprit to justice. Apart from the bullet, there was little forensic evidence of value at the scene. Detectives had to grapple from the beginning with the question of why the crime had been committed.

The problem was that the murder seemed inexplicable. Investigators had to consider no fewer than six categories of possible motive, some of them quite obscure. The immediate focus was on the victim's personal life. Most murders are carried out by people who are known to the victim, particularly partners. Dando was engaged to be married to a highly respected doctor, but the police had to consider whether there was a secret within the relationship that would have prompted the killing. Inquiries revealed that the couple's relationship was happy and the doctor was soon ruled out as a suspect.

The impending marriage might, however, have prompted a former partner of either Dando or the doctor to commit the crime in a jealous rage. It was also conceivable that the spark for the crime was irrational jealousy on the part of one of the doctor's patients. Although the MO of the gunman seemed inconsistent with a rage killing, it was possible that an assassin had been hired. There was no evidence that either Dando or her partner had been harassed by a former lover or patient, but the police painstakingly traced anyone who had had personal relationships with them. They went back to Dando's earliest romances and talked to many of the doctor's patients, some of whom had developed a strong attachment to him because of his caring and professional manner. Over time, however, the many possible suspects were gradually eliminated from the inquiry. A third

1 Barry George, the man accused of murdering TV personality Jill Dando.
2 Closed-circuit film showing Jill Dando shopping in London, taken 40 minutes before she was murdered outside her home in Fulham.

possibility was that Dando's celebrity status was irrelevant and that she had been killed after confronting a would-be burglar at her home. Murders are often committed by mistake, and this possibility was studied in depth. No fewer than 191 closed-circuit TV cameras in the neighborhood were scrutinized to see whether there was any sign that Dando had been followed. A picture of her movements during her last day was built up, but her money and possessions had not been touched and there was no evidence to suggest that it was a burglar who had crept up behind her and fired the fatal shot.

Dando was best known as a host of the BBC television program *Crimewatch UK*, in which police appealed to viewers for assistance in solving crimes. So another possible motive for the murder was that a criminal had been so incensed with the program for having him or one of his associates arrested, that a contract killing had been organized and committed. The police needed to check on the background of all the criminals featured by Dando and the program's other hosts. Up to thirty people with clear links to the program were investigated and eliminated. Convicted contract killers were also questioned about likely suspects. A suggestion that a notorious crime gang might have been responsible was even explored, only to be discarded. Apart from the lack of credible suspects, it was not clear why a criminal would seek to assassinate a television personality rather than a police officer or whoever had provided information leading to his arrest. In any event, it is unusual for professional assassins to shoot a victim only once—the victim might survive—or to use a homemade gun, as Dando's killer had.

A further possible motive seemed at first to be ludicrous, but demanded careful consideration.

Dando had presented a television appeal for aid for Kosovan refugees and a few days later NATO fired a cruise missile at a television station owned by a relative of Slobodan Milosovic, then the Serbian leader, killing seventeen people. It was suggested that a Serb assassin might have killed Ms Dando on the instructions of the notorious war criminal Arkan. Telephone calls to BBC television following the murder claimed that the shooting was in revenge for the NATO bombing, and that marks on the bullet were similar to those seen on ammunition used in Serbia. Police investigations established that Serbian gangs had killed journalists, but that they usually used knives, wore masks, and inflicted a large number of wounds to act as a deterrent to others.

The sixth and final possibility was that the killer was an obsessed stalker who had murdered Dando to stop her marrying, to gain notoriety, or for some other irrational reason. Shortly before her death, Dando had appeared on the front cover of the BBC magazine *Radio Times* wearing a tight-fitting leather jumpsuit, and it was possible that this had attracted the attention of someone who had an unhealthy fascination for her. The investigating team discovered no fewer than one hundred and forty people who had some kind of obsession with Dando. Although she appeared to have been expertly executed, a killing by a single shot from a makeshift weapon was more consistent with a deranged stalker than a hired killer. On the other hand, although stalking is commonplace, there had not been a single case in the U.K. of a celebrity being murdered by a stalker.

This bewildering array of possible motives made the search for the culprit exceptionally time-consuming, with the added complication of public demand for a quick arrest and the need to investigate dead-ends introduced into the inquiry by time-wasting troublemakers.

As a result of all the complications, the investigation involved:

- **taking more than 2,400 statements**
- **interviewing more than 5,000 people**
- **examining more than 2,000 documents and more than 3,600 items of property**
- **identifying more than 80,000 mobile phone numbers that had been in use in the vicinity of the crime**
- **speaking to nearly 500 people whose names appeared in the victim's personal organiser**
- **examining about 14,000 e-mails received by BBC Television before and after the murder**

The investigation reportedly cost over two million U.K. pounds (roughly three million U.S. dollars), but despite devoting massive resources to the inquiry, uncertainty about the motive meant that seven months passed before the police decided to concentrate primarily on the theory that the killer was a stalker. On the second day of the investigation, the name of a well-known local eccentric, Barry George, who lived near Dando, had been reported to the detectives. But descriptions and timings of possible sightings of the killer from witnesses in the vicinity of the crime did not seem to correspond with George's appearance and movements. As a result, he was given a low priority in the inquiry and not asked to provide a witness statement until almost a year after the murder. When his home was searched, minute forensic evidence was discovered that would ultimately be crucial to securing his conviction. When he stood trial, George's defense team argued that the "Serbian revenge" motive was the most likely explanation for the crime.

Given that forensic evidence was in short supply, and that the motive remained unclear, many commentators during the trial doubted whether the jury would convict. When a guilty verdict was returned, the judge said in sentencing Barry George to life imprisonment: "Why you did it will never be known." The absence of a comprehensible motive is a key feature of the arguments of those who maintain that George was innocent and that his conviction was a miscarriage of justice that has allowed the real culprit to go free.

UNDERSTANDING MOTIVE

As the Dando case shows so vividly, homicide investigators need to consider both rational and irrational motives for a crime as well as the possibility of an accidental killing. At the start of a homicide investigation it is vital to keep an open mind about the killer's motivation: failure to do so can prove disastrous.

Early assumptions made by English police investigating the White House Farm murders in 1985 risked compromising the investigation. The bodies of five members of the Bamber family were found dead at the farm. One of the corpses was that of Sheila Caffell, a woman with a history of mental problems. A .22 rifle, which proved to be the murder weapon, lay across her body. It appeared to investigators who arrived at the scene that a deranged Sheila had killed her adoptive parents and her two children, and had then committed suicide. Further investigation, however, revealed that Jeremy Bamber, who had called the police to the scene, had committed the crimes for financial gain. But confusion about the reasons for the killings, and the belated search for evidence linking Bamber to the crimes, have left a question mark over Bamber's conviction, especially since he has consistently protested his innocence.

It is true, in general, that people's behavior reflects their personalities. This is as true of victims as of perpetrators. The specific features of a particular crime may be unusual, but the patterns of behavior associated with the crime may be more common and understandable to investigators who, with the aid of crime profilers, seek to understand the events that led up to the murder.

Various attempts have been made to categorize possible motives for murder. Occasionally, gender-based distinctions are drawn. Statistically, for example, only a very small proportion of all serial killers are female. The British criminologist Brian Lane, in *The Encyclopaedia of Women Killers* (1994), has suggested that most women who kill fall into two broad categories: Those who want to kill and those who do not.

The classification of motives for murder that has best stood the test of time was developed by another British writer, F. Tennyson Jesse, in her ground-breaking study *Murder and Its Motives* (1924). She argued that in murder there are differences of both degree and, crucially most important, of kind. Understanding those differences helps investigators classify the psychological components of the crime. Jesse did not fully appreciate the potential of psychological profiling as an aid in the detection of murder, but her theory that every murder falls into one of six broad classes remains valid to this day. She accepted that a murder may belong to two or even more of the classes and she defined the classes so broadly that each covered a range of motivations. The categories that she identified were:

> murder for gain
> murder for revenge
> murder for elimination
> murder for jealousy
> murder from conviction
> murder for the lust of killing

Brian Lane has argued that there is a seventh category: murder for thrill of the act. But this can be treated as murder for the lust of killing. Another possible category is that of the "hate crime," killing for racist or homophobic reasons.

Jesse was not a scientist, and her study of criminal motivation is flawed by a number of questionable generalizations. She did, however, possess an acute understanding of human behavior and maintained that the classes she had identified covered a wide range of culprits.

MURDER FOR GAIN

Murder for gain might be a crime committed for only a small amount of money by a stupid or desperate killer. A murder for gain may also be disguised as another type of killing. A strange example occurred in South Africa in 1961, when Marthinus Rossouw claimed that he murdered Baron Dietrich Van Schauroth at the latter's request. The case that Jesse chose to illustrate the gain motive was that of the nineteenth-century doctor, William Palmer, who poisoned at least fourteen people before being brought to justice.

1 Sheila Caffell with her children. Her mental state caused confusion as to whether or not she had killed her family and then committed suicide.
2 Alice Cummins outside the courthouse in N.Y.
3 Edmund Cummins comforts his wife after she was charged with murdering her daughter.
4 Denise Labbe was sentenced to life in prison for the murder of her infant child.

IDENTIFYING CRIMINAL CHARACTERISTICS

In 1879, a French clerk, Alphonse Bertillon, reported on a system for identifying criminals by reference to their physical characteristics. His starting point was the theory that no two people have precisely the same body measurements in combination. Bertillon listed fourteeen measurements, including the length and circumference of the head, and the length of the fingers and feet, which taken as a whole made the chances of duplication in two individuals extremely remote. This system of anthropometry, or "man measurement," came to be known as "Bertillonage" and was widely used. Encouraged by the enthusiasm for his work, Bertillon began to instruct detectives in the technique of *portrait parlé* ("word portrait"). In Italy, *portrait parlé* was developed to take account of other characteristics such as body movement and patterns of behavior. However, Bertillon's reputation was damaged by his hostility toward fingerprinting and by his testimony in the Dreyfus affair. He gave evidence that Captain Alfred Dreyfus had written a letter sent by an unknown traitor and as a result Dreyfus spent twelve years on the infamous Devil's Island for a crime he did not commit until the real traitor was correctly identified.

Although fingerprinting superseded Bertillonage, the *portrait parlé* concept paved the way for new techniques such as the Identikit system, devised by Hugh C. McDonald of the Los Angeles Police Department, and based on face types. The first Identikit field pack contained five hundred coded and numbered transparencies, each bearing a drawing of a single facial component—but not ears, since it was thought that witnesses often never see a criminal's ears or at least don't remember them correctly. Identikit transparencies were coded by letter or number so that they could easily be transferred from one location to another.

Even more elaborate was the Photofit system devised by Jacques Penry. This is a face building system that, instead of the line drawings associated with Identikit, is based on photographs of sets of facial components: forehead/hair, eyes, nose/mouth, and lower jaw/chin. The system was introduced by Penry in Britain in 1971 and has found favor with law enforcement agencies around the world.

Identification techniques continue to evolve, although even relatively unsophisticated methods such as line-ups and sketches by police artists still have a part to play in modern crime detection. But new technology offers some of the more exciting possibilities. Voiceprinting is a way of comparing voices electronically by measuring resonance, pitch, and volume. These qualities are traced onto paper, not unlike a lie-detector readout. The theory is that every person has a unique mode of speech, although opinions as to the accuracy of identification by voiceprint vary and voiceprint evidence is not always accepted by courts. The evolution of computer graphics technology has, however, made for more accurate portrayals of suspects, through the ability to create an image with depth, color, and texture not available with the Identikit or Photofit systems. The three-dimensional images produced by videofit (or e-fit) can

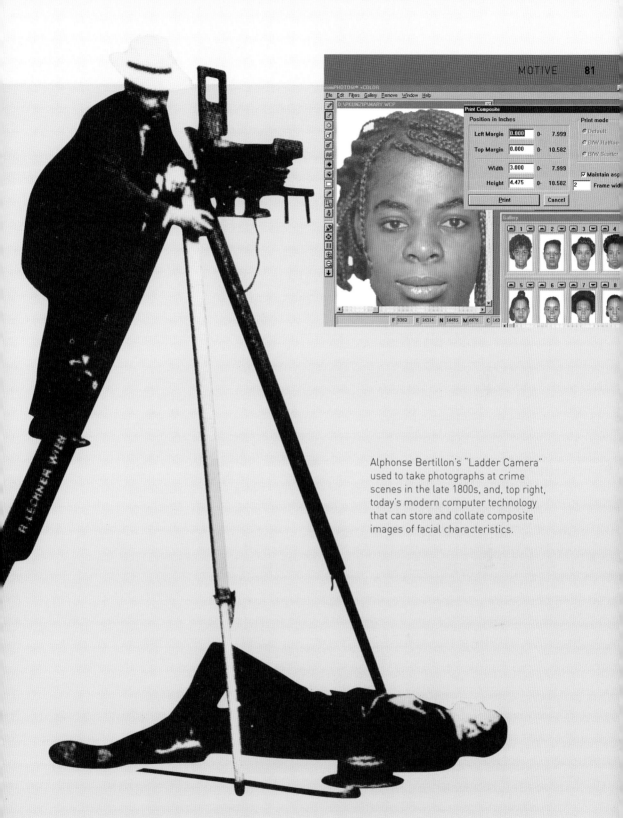

comPHOTOfit® +COLOR

File Edit Filters Gallery Remove Window Help

D:\PKUNZIP\MARY.WCP

Print Composite

Position in Inches

Left Margin [0.000]   0- 7.999

Top Margin [0.000]   0- 10.582

Width [3.000]   0- 7.999

Height [4.475]   0- 10.582

Print mode
○ Default
○ B/W Halftone
○ B/W Scatter

☑ Maintain asp

Frame wid [2]

Print   Cancel

Gallery

F 8382   E 16314   N 16485   M 6676   C 163

Alphonse Bertillon's "Ladder Camera"
used to take photographs at crime
scenes in the late 1800s, and, top right,
today's modern computer technology
that can store and collate composite
images of facial characteristics.

produce amazing likenesses. Even so, the accuracy of any image—computer-based or not—will ultimately depend on the ability of the witnesses to describe facial characteristics, together with the skill of the identification system.

Long before his arrest, he had been the subject of rumors about the deaths of members of his family, but the combination of his respectable profession and his apparently charming disposition and relative youth (he was only thirty one when he was hanged) helped him to continue his criminal career until there was overwhelming evidence that he had committed murder repeatedly in order to stave off financial pressures caused by his addiction to gambling. Jesse acknowledged that some of the deaths of which Palmer was suspected—those of several of his illegitimate children—belong to the class of "murder for elimination," and this is no more than an acknowledgement of the reality that murderers often have mixed motives.

MURDER FOR REVENGE

The case that Jesse chose to illustrate murder for revenge was that of Constance Kent, a sixteen-year-old girl who, in 1860, took revenge on a hated stepmother by killing her four-year-old stepbrother. Again, the classification of the murder is not precise, since Constance Kent was evidently also afflicted by jealousy. A typical revenge killing was the murder, in 1995, of three British children, Terry, Nicola, and Alison Good, in an arson attack on their home. The killer was Fred Heyworth, who was evidently seeking revenge on the children's mother, Beverley Good. He suspected Beverley of poisoning the mind of his wife (her sister) against him and retaliated by pouring gasoline through the mail slot of her house and setting fire to it.

MURDER FOR ELIMINATION

Jesse defined true murder for elimination as the removal of someone because his or her continued existence is an inconvenience or a danger. She said that "murders of this class are interesting, in

that they are of necessity calculated affairs," even though the motive may spring from passion and gave as an example a nineteenth-century noble Breton family, the Quérangals, who presented "a wonderful picture of a whole decadent family ready to remove those who inconvenienced them." Typically, contract killings involve murders for elimination, as do many love-triangle cases, such as the murder by Ruth Snyder and Judd Gray of Ruth's husband Albert in Long Island, New York, in 1927. Gangland killings also fall under this heading. Other cases are more complicated; for example the murder of the two children of Alice and Edmund Cummins in New York in 1965. Alice Cummins was convicted of first-degree murder in 1968, but the verdict was overturned on appeal. She was convicted again in 1971, although her sentence was later reduced on yet another appeal. Evidence suggested that she "preferred to see her children dead than allow her husband to get custody of them." The need to kill was more obviously acute in the case of the Canadian financier Albert Walker (see pages 102-3). He had exchanged identities with Ronald Platt in order to escape the consequences of his business frauds. When Platt's continued existence threatened his security, Walker murdered him.

MURDER FOR JEALOUSY

Jean Harris killed her lover Dr. Herman Tarnower because she was embittered as a result of his affair with Lynne Tryforos. The crucial evidence at her trial came from what was to be called the "Scarsdale Letter," which Harris had sent to Tarnower immediately before setting off to confront him. She referred to her rival as "a vicious, adulterous psychotic" and said that she did not care "even if the slut comes—indeed, I don't care if she pops naked out of a cake with her tits frosted with chocolate!" The whole letter was in the same vein. It was a vituperative rant that included a claim that she had taken money from Tarnower's wallet to buy clothes to replace those which, she alleged, had been damaged by her rival. The letter was immensely damaging to Harris's defense, since it effectively wrecked the picture that her legal team had tried to paint of a respectable woman who would never stoop to deliberately murdering her lover. It is always difficult for a jury to know how much weight to give to evidence that appears to cast light on what is going on inside the mind of the accused. In most cases, however, dramatic material such as the Scarsdale Letter is bound to have a major impact on the way in which jurors assess the prosecution's case.

Jealousy takes many forms, as two British cases show. In 1890, Mary Eleanor Pearcey killed the wife of a man with whom she was infatuated as well as the couple's eighteen-month-old baby. Jesse compares this case to a story by Zola: "Mrs Pearcey must have been a woman not unlike Thérèse Raquin in her remorselessness, eaten up with her own desires, and with all the persistence of an animal with its nose on the trail." The second case involves the celebrated playwright Joe Orton who had an affair with a writer, Kenneth Halliwell, seven years his senior. In the early years of the relationship Halliwell saw himself as Orton's mentor. Halliwell was possessive and, as Orton's fame grew and his own career stalled, he became depressed and angry. Orton exacerbated matters by failing to acknowledge Halliwell's support and by recording, in a diary to which Halliwell had access, details of a string of casual gay affairs. In August 1967, Halliwell fatally smashed Orton's head with

a hammer, and then took an overdose of barbiturates. Their bodies were discovered by a chauffeur who had come to drive Orton to a meeting with film executives who had bought the screen rights to one of his plays.

MURDER FROM CONVICTION

This category of homicidal motives includes politically inspired assassinations and terrorist killings. According to John Douglas in *The Anatomy of Motive* (1999) assassins tend to be loners with poor self-esteem who often suffer from paranoia. In *Encyclopaedia of Assassinations* (1993), Carl Sifakis identifies two classes of assassination: "antiestablishment murders" and "establishment murders." The former includes the crimes of insane killers and dedicated revolutionaries; the latter refers to assassination to achieve political ends. The murder of political figures often provokes conspiracy theories: President John F. Kennedy's murder, for example. The attempted murder of President Ronald Reagan by John W. Hinckley in 1981 was particularly unique. Hinckley was obsessed with the actress Jodie Foster, whom he had seen in the movie *Taxi Driver*, in which a character played by Robert DeNiro plans to murder a presidential candidate. The way in which fiction and real life play off one other is underscored by the fact that the DeNiro character was loosely based on Arthur Bremer, who tried to kill Governor George Wallace in Laurel, Maryland, in 1972. Detectives found an unsent letter in Hinckley's room in which he spoke, presumably to Jodie Foster, of his plan to murder the president, although he said "I would abandon this idea of getting Reagan in a second if I could only win your heart and live out the rest of my life with you." Hinckley was found to be insane and was committed to a mental institution. Bremer had also articulated his feelings through a detailed diary, as did Sirhan Sirhan, who murdered Senator Robert Kennedy in Los Angeles in 1968. It is common for assassins, who are typically social loners, to express their true feelings in secret writings.

Killings by or on behalf of cults such as Japan's Aum cult may seem to be types of murders through conviction, although in truth the principal motive is often financial gain or the elimination of a perceived threat. Serial killers occasionally claim to be acting out of conviction. Peter Sutcliffe, the Yorkshire Ripper, is typical. At the time of his arrest he told police that he had started killing prostitutes out of anger when he was cheated by one, but his story in court was that he had been following instructions from God. The prosecution argued that Sutcliffe was a sexual sadist who murdered for the love of killing. The jury was not convinced by Sutcliffe's defense and found him guilty of thirteen murders and seven attempted murders.

MURDER FOR THE LUST OF KILLING

The Chicago teenagers Leopold and Loeb "wanted the new thrill of killing," in Jesse's words, so they murdered a fourteen-year-old boy. Not surprisingly, so unusual a crime has attracted the attention of many writers. The case was turned into the play *Rope* by Patrick Hamilton (famously filmed by Alfred Hitchcock) and the novel *Compulsion* (1956) by Meyer Levin. The Leopold and Loeb case has been described as an example of a "motiveless" or "experimental" murder, but it is perhaps best interpreted as a form of lust or thrill killing. The same is true of the crimes of Dennis Nilsen, a London-based government worker who

in 1983 confessed to murdering fifteen young, mostly down-and-out, homosexuals. His MO was to pick up the victims in a bar and take them home, where he would strangle them, usually with a tie, after they had fallen asleep following a bout of heavy drinking. He boiled the heads of some of the victims in a cooking pot. At first he kept the corpses under the floorboards. Later, he cut them up and disposed of the remains in various crude ways, including keeping them around the house in sacks and stuffing them into the drains. Defense psychiatrists claimed that Nilsen was paranoid or that he treated people as figments of fantasy. The jury found him guilty of murder, rejecting the argument that his mental capacity was sufficiently impaired for the case to be treated as one of multiple manslaughter. Brian Masters wrote a book about Nilsen, *Killing for Company* (1985), which contended that Nilsen committed murder to stave off loneliness: an interesting but debatable hypothesis.

Jesse chose to illustrate this category of murderer with the nineteenth-century strychnine poisoner, Dr. Neill Cream, who took pleasure from reflecting upon the suffering of his victims and who, according to one improbable theory, may also have been Jack the Ripper. She made little attempt to analyze the motivations of serial killers such as Peter Kürten, the Monster of Dusseldorf, who "murdered from bloodlust," Joseph Vacher, the French vagrant who wandered the countryside stealing and killing, or Fritz Haarman, the Butcher

1 The Yorkshire Ripper, Peter Sutcliffe, (under a jacket) is led from court following his trial.
2 The attempted assassination of President Ronald Reagan in Washington DC in March 1981.

THEN AND NOW

OFFENDER PROFILING

The idea that some people are born with criminal tendencies is age-old. Charles Darwin's theory of evolution prompted developments in the science of anthropology that were taken up by criminologists. The Italian Cesare Lombroso sought to relate criminal conduct to criminal personality that could be identified by "anthropometry," that is, classification based on physical characteristics. In his book *L'Uomo Delinquente*, translated as "Criminal Man," Lombroso attempted to describe criminal types by reference to criminal characteristics. According to Lombroso, assassins had prominent jaws, widely separated cheekbones, and thick dark hair; murderers were taller, heavier, and stronger than thieves. Although much of the detail of Lombroso's work seems misguided today, his approach paved the way for an increasingly thoughtful study of criminal behavior. In 1888, Dr. Bond wrote to the head of the London CID suggesting likely characteristics for the elusive Jack the Ripper: "He would be solitary and eccentric in his habits, also he is most likely to be a man without regular occupation … possibly living among respectable persons who have some knowledge of his character and habits and who may have grounds for the suspicions that he is not quite right in his mind at times." The failure of police to ever identify the Ripper murders means that the accuracy of Bond's assessment cannot be proved, but it does seem plausible. In the mid 1950s, Dr. James A. Brussel provided a detailed description of New York's so-called Mad Bomber as a "single man between forty and fifty years old, introvert. Unsocial but not anti-social. Skilled mechanic … Not interested in women. High school graduate … Religious. Might react violently at work when criticised." When the culprit, George Metsky, was apprehended, Brussel's account proved accurate. Later, Brussel also correctly profiled the Boston Strangler, Albert DeSalvo, recognizing that despite differences in the individual attacks of this case, it was certainly the work of one man.

In the 1970s, a more structured approach to profiling emerged. Serial killing cases were increasing and traditional homicide investigation techniques seemed inadequate. A Behavioral Science Unit was set up at the FBI's National Academy at Quantico, where agents developed a methodical system of profiling. The Violent Criminal Apprehension Program (VICAP) was established as a central information system for collecting and analyzing reports on criminals nationwide, with a view toward identifying patterns of serial crime.

Psychologists with profiling expertise have played an important role in many investigations, and an understanding of the thought processes of murderers has been improved as a result of in-depth interviewing of serial killers such as John Wayne Gacy and Ted Bundy. The emphasis is increasingly on the practical rather than the academic: a new breed of homicide detectives is emerging, expert in both

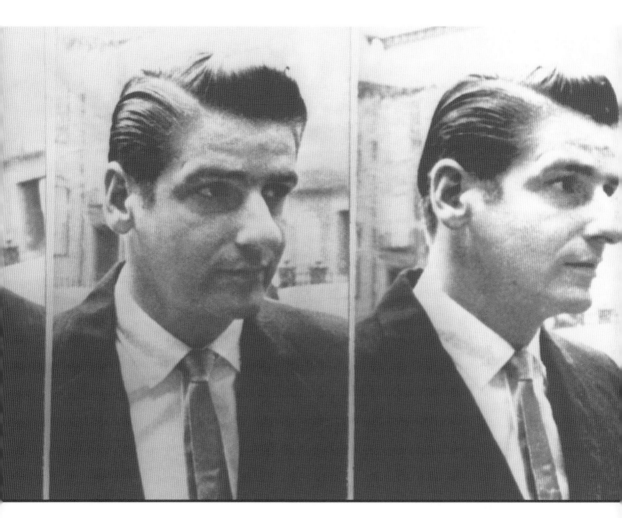

Albert DeSalvo, a thirty-four-year-old mental patient, was tried for the murder of eleven women in eastern Massachusetts. Using offender profiling methods, he was successfully linked to his victims.

investigative psychology and the latest information technology. The influence of profiling has prompted a change in approach to homicide detection. As well as searching for a particular physical clue that has a direct link to an individual, the identification of various patterns in behavior has also become a major focal point of investigations. The recognition that behavioral analysis can help detectives to identify likely suspects has increased the importance of interviews and interviewing techniques. The net is closing in on serial killers whose identification had been impossible with more traditional methods.

of Hanover, who was responsible for the deaths of at least twenty-seven boys and young men from 1919 to 1924 and sold meat from their bodies as food. Serial killing is, as these cases show, far from new. But comprehension of this type of crime has grown over the years, as an upsurge in serial killings in the U.S. has been met with growing sophistication in criminal analysis, the result of the work of the FBI's Behavioral Science Unit as well as that of psychological profilers who have studied patterns in serial crime.

In *The New Encyclopaedia of Serial Killers* (1996), Brian Lane and Wilfred Gregg usefully identify four main types of motivation seen in serial killings:

- **visionaries who respond to voices in their heads and other instructions**
- **missionaries who seek to clean up society**
- **hedonists who enjoy the act of killing**
- **power seekers who enjoy having control over the life and death of others**

Hedonists can further be classified as follows:

- **lust killers motivated by the quest for sexual gratification**
- **thrill killers whose prime aim is to enjoy the experience of killing**
- **gain killers, where the act of killing is incidental to some other motive, such as greed, as in the case of George Joseph Smith, the British "Brides in the Bath" killer**

Serial killers are one of the three groups of people who commit multiple murders. The other two groups, mass murderers and spree killers, overlap. A mass murderer kills several people at random at one particular time and in one particular place.

Examples include Colin Ferguson, who boarded a New York train in 1993 and gunned down five people, injuring nineteen others; and Thomas Hamilton, who killed sixteen children and their teacher at Dunblane, Scotland, in 1996. Spree killers kill several people over a slightly longer period of time, and often in several locations. Andrew Cunanan, whose victims included the designer Gianni Versace, who was murdered outside his home in Miami's South Beach in 1997, was atypical of spree killers in that he was also a sexual predator. He began as a serial killer, but his crimes turned into a wild spree as he killed for the thrill of it or because he was angry or wanted something. Mass and spree murderers tend to have little interest in escape or their own safety and often, like Hamilton and Cunanan, commit suicide. One interpretation of this form of crime is that it is an extended act of self-destruction. These killers are usually male, white, and in their 30s or 40s. They are often obsessed with firearms (the usual weapon of choice for their murders) and have had lives characterized by under-achievement and resentment.

In contrast, serial killers commit a sequence of murders, often increasing in frequency over a considerable period of time. The crimes usually continue until the culprit is apprehended or killed. The killings are usually one-on-one, although a

1 Weapons used by murderer Denis Nilsen including a pot used to boil some of their remains.
2 Andrew Cunanan with a friend, before he started his run of spree killings.
3 The scene of the murder in Miami beach of Gianni Versace by Andrew Cunanan.

number of killer couples such as the Lonely Hearts Killers, Martha Beck and Raymond Fernandez, have worked together, while David Berkowitz, aka Son of Sam, often targeted couples. In serial crimes it is rare for there to be a connection between culprit and victim: the latter is often simply in the wrong place at the wrong time. Serial killings are frequently committed with much more violence than is necessary to ensure the death of the victim and are often sexually motivated and result in mutilation of the corpse. The killer's MO tends to be consistent throughout the series and each crime scene may yield a psychological "calling card" of that particular offender.

THE CRIMINAL MIND

For many years, psychiatrists—and crime writers—have struggled, often with limited success, to understand the mindset of those who commit horrific murders. Most experts now accept that there is a distinction between killers who suffer from a psychosis and those who used to be known as psychopaths or sociopaths and who are now said to be suffering from an antisocial personality disorder.

It is still unclear what sparks the onset of psychosis. It may be significant that many of those who have committed appalling murders have suffered head injuries earlier in their lives.

During a psychotic episode, the person's working memory, or ability to navigate through life, is impaired. MRI scans of the brain can provide valuable information. The scans not only display the brain's anatomy, but also show its physiological activity: when any part of the brain is stimulated, instruments light up. The way in which this activity differs between people with a psychiatric impairment and those who are mentally healthy may point the way to better diagnosis and treatment. There is already evidence that psychosis is treatable through medication.

Unlike a person suffering a psychotic episode, a person with an antisocial personality disorder may seem sane while being capable of acts of extreme inhumanity: according to some estimates, perhaps ninety percent of serial killers have such personality disorders. They often lack conscience and live by their own rules. They may, like the serial killer Ted Bundy, possess considerable charm, but be highly egocentric and lacking in empathy. In particular, they have no concern for the suffering of their victims.

There is as yet no proven treatment for personality disorders; it has even been suggested that group therapy treatment makes the disorder worser, since the psychopath sees the sessions as a way to refine his or her homicidal techniques through absorbing extra information on human frailties and how best to exploit them.

1 A magnetic resonance imaging (MRI) scan of a human head uses pulses of radio waves to form "slice" images that are compiled into colored three-dimensional images by computer.
2 Ted Bundy (center), surrounded by members of his defense team, was sentenced to death for a series of horrendous killings.

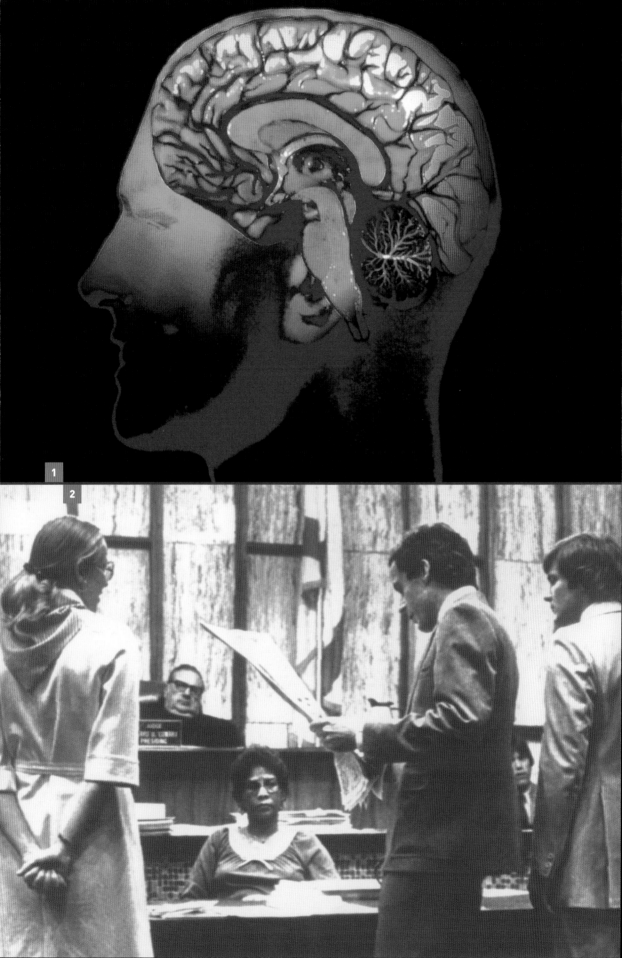

A DEADLY DUO

By the time the handsome and wealthy twenty-eight-year-old Paul Bernardo had married Karla Homolka in a lavish ceremony at a church in Niagara-on-the-Lake in 1991, the couple had already been responsible for the death of Karla's sister. Prior to that, Bernardo had committed a series of rapes in Toronto between 1987 and 1990, attributed in the Canadian press to the Scarborough Rapist. The rapist's MO was to come up behind women late at night, often when they got off buses, and overpower them. As he carried out the attacks he verbally abused the women and threatened to kill them. An artist's composite drawing of the rapist prompted someone who knew Bernardo to contact the police. Bernardo cooperated with the detectives who visited him and provided blood, hair, and saliva samples, but DNA testing was in its infancy and the samples were not processed.

Bernardo had trained as an accountant but taken up an alternative career as a cigarette smuggler. Not long after his relationship with Homolka began, he persuaded her to help him to rape her fifteen-year-old sister Tammy. Homolka worked in a veterinary clinic and decided that they should use halothane, an anesthetic given to animals before surgery, to subdue Tammy. As the couple assaulted her, Tammy choked to death. An ambulance was called and authorities accepted the incident as an accident. It seems clear that Tammy's death was unintentional, but shortly after the couple married, Bernardo kidnaped a girl named Leslie Mahaffy, took her home, and started to abuse her. As with Tammy, he recorded the assault on video. Homolka woke and Bernardo persuaded her to help him in the attack on Leslie. Two weeks later, Leslie's body parts were found in Lake Gibson, encased in concrete.

The next body to be found was that of another teenager, Kristen French. Homolka lured her to a car, by asking for directions, so that Bernardo could force her at knifepoint into the back seat. She was subjected to a lengthy sexual ordeal, again recorded on video, before being killed. Her body was found in a ditch but had not been dismembered, so at first investigators did not believe that her murder was connected with that of Leslie Mahaffy. Three weeks later the body of a third girl, Terri Anderson, was found in the water at Port Dalhousie, but murder was not at first suspected; examination of the corpse was hampered by the fact that it had been in the water for six months.

Eventually Homolka confessed to the police. Bernardo had consistently beaten and degraded her and her lawyers negotiated a plea bargain that resulted in her receiving a twelve-year sentence with eligibility for early parole. Bernardo was convicted on all the kidnaping, rape, and murder charges that he faced and, though he will be eligible for parole after twenty-five years, it is unlikely that he will be released. The relatively lenient sentence on Homolka reflects the reality that she was subjugated to the will of a sexual sadist who charmed her into a relationship and, once she was emotionally dependent upon him and terrified of incurring his wrath, isolated her from family and friends and used her to help him act out his fantasies.

1 Karla Homolka, influenced by the sexual sadist, Paul Bernado, walks to court to learn her own fate.
2 Paul Bernado in a car on the way to court to hear sentence.

EXPERIMENTS IN DEATH

In May 1924, the naked body of a fourteen-year-old boy, Bobby Franks, was found stuffed into a drainpipe in Chicago. The boy's parents had already been telephoned to say that he had been kidnaped and they had received a ransom note typed on an Underwood typewriter. An unusual pair of eyeglasses found at the crime scene was identified as belonging to a young man of nineteen, Nathan Leopold. Samples of his typing were also found, and matched the ransom note. He confessed, implicating an eighteen-year-old friend, Richard Loeb, who had already offered to help the police in their investigation. Loeb then also confessed. Their stories were similar except that, at first, each accused the other of killing Bobby. Loeb later acknowledged that he was responsible.

The culprits came from wealthy German-Jewish families. Leopold was exceptionally intelligent, short, and near-sighted. Loeb was the dominant partner in the relationship and was handsome, daring, and charismatic. Leopold adored him and took masochistic pleasure in describing himself as Loeb's slave. Loeb stole things, supposedly to prove his superiority—in the Nietzschean tradition—to ordinary mortals and conventional morality. He suggested that the two of them should commit the murder of a child as a further sign of their superiority and then pretend that they had kidnaped their victim and collect a ransom.

Bobby Franks was a distant cousin of Loeb's. They invited him to come for a ride in a hired car. Leopold drove and Loeb, sitting in the back with the boy, hit him on the head with a heavy chisel, put a gag in his mouth, and kept hitting until he was dead. They took the corpse to a culvert, stripped it, poured acid over the face, and pushed it into the drainpipe.

Clarence Darrow, the famous defense attorney and passionate opponent of the death penalty, defended the pair. Since there was no denying their joint venture into homicide, his task was to save their lives. This he achieved, partly thanks to a long and emotional closing speech and partly due to the youth of his clients.

In 1936, Loeb was slashed with a razor by a fellow prisoner in a homosexual brawl and died of his wounds. Leopold was released from prison in 1958 and lived for another thirteen years. He sued the novelist Meyer Levin, whose book *Compulsion* fictionalized the case. The claim of alleged invasion of privacy was thrown out and it has been theorized that Leopold's anger was aroused by the book's unsubtle Freudian suggestion that the killing was sexually motivated: the chisel symbolizing a penis and the drainpipe a vagina. The murder of Bobby is sometimes described as motiveless or as having been committed for kicks, but a sexual motive seems probable, although the crime writer Julian Symons, himself of Jewish descent, theorized that the duo's crime "may be traced to the feeling of many Jews that they are unacceptable to the society in which they live."

1 Nathan Leopold and Richard Loeb (second and fourth from right) with their families and lawyers.
2 Leopold leaves prison on parole for his part in the thrill slaying of Bobby Franks.

THE LADY KILLER

The classic serial murderer killer is profiled as a white male in his 30s or 40s. Aileen Wuornos fit the pattern for age and race but not for gender. She is regarded as the first American female serial killer.

In December 1989, the decomposed body of a fifty-one-year-old electrician, Richard Mallory, was found wrapped in a carpet in woods outside Ormond Beach, Florida. He had been shot in the head and chest with a .22 handgun. Within a year, five more victims were discovered in similar circumstances. Each was a white, middle-aged heterosexual man who had apparently been killed in or near his vehicle close to a state highway and whose corpse had been concealed in nearby scrub or woodland. Some were partially dressed, but although there was evidence that certain victims had been involved in a sexual encounter shortly before death, there were no signs that their bodies had been sexually abused or beaten. In each case, money, possessions, and the victim's vehicle had been taken. The cars had been abandoned, with the driver's seat pushed forward, suggesting that a short person had needed to reach for the pedals. The MO was consistent: the same handgun was used in each murder. FBI profilers suggested that the culprit was a woman.

On July 4, 1990, witnesses had seen a car skidding off the road and two women fleeing from it. The car belonged to a missing man named Peter Seims. At first, this incident was not connected with the Florida highway killings, but a link was later made and police issued a sketch artist's drawing of the women. The names of Lee Wuornos, a prostitute, and her lover Tyria J. Moore came up and Wuornos's thumbprint was found on a pawn ticket given for several items belonging to Richard Mallory. Wuornos was arrested and Moore helped the police to secure further evidence. Wuornos made a videotaped confession in which she claimed she had gone into the woods with each victim to have sex in return for cash, and that each man had attacked or tried to rape her, compelling her to kill him in self-defense. Wuornos was to be tried separately for each crime and her lawyers argued that the jury in the Mallory case should hear evidence about the other murders, but the judge rejected their request. The jury was not told that Mallory had once been sent to prison for rape and Wuornos was convicted and sentenced to death in the electric chair. Wuornos's motive remains unclear. The prosecution may have been right in saying that she killed primarily for financial gain. Another theory is that she was revenging herself upon men because she had been raped and abused in the past, and this may in part explain the crimes. It is also possible that, in some cases at least, her claim that her victims attacked or threatened her was true; it is understandable, however, that the jury was unwilling to believe that she had been so unfortunate on so many occasions in the course of one year.

Portrait of a female killer: Aileen Wuornos testifying in front of the court.

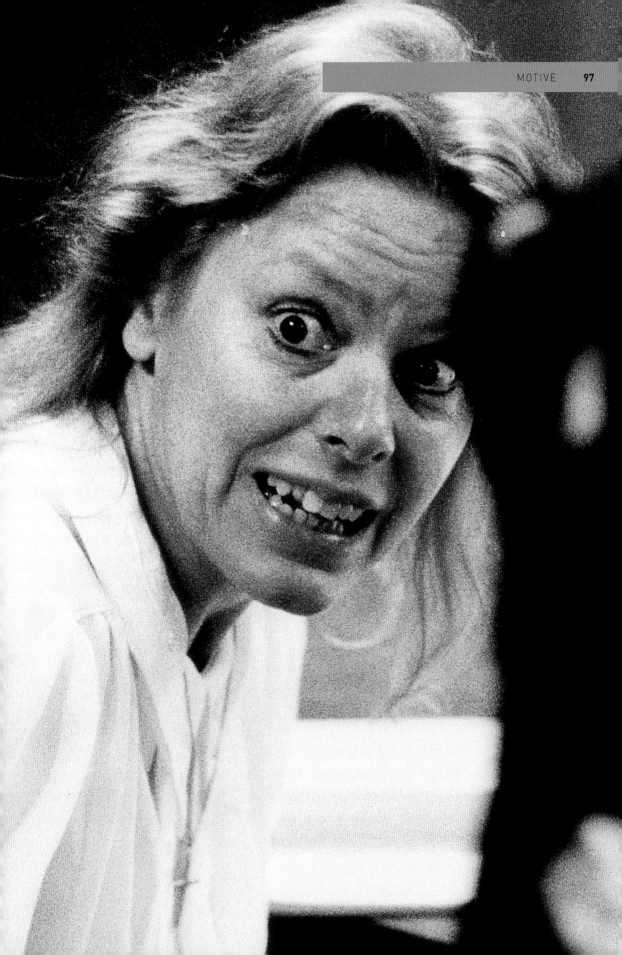

A KILLING SPREE

Port Arthur in Tasmania was once the site of a prison colony. Today it is a major tourist attraction. On the afternoon of Sunday April 28, 1996, the Broad Arrow café was busy. A young man with long fair hair finished eating on the balcony, then moved back inside. He started watching an Asian couple at a nearby table and then took an AR 15 semi-automatic rifle out of a bag and shot both the man and the woman. He turned his fire on other diners, and as terrified people tried to hide, he killed another eighteen, wounding several others. Leaving the café and driving off, he continued to shoot, claiming still more victims. He then stopped at an inn called Seascape Cottage, took a male hostage, and set fire to a BMW he had stolen.

The police were summoned and sealed off the area before the Special Operations Group took over. As they took up positions around the building, shots were fired at them. Poor radio reception hampered police communications and lack of suitable cover around the building caused police to call in a team of special negotiators. Questioning revealed that the gunman was twenty-eight-year-old Martin Bryant, who was believed to possess several firearms. Senior negotiator Sergeant Terry McCarthy talked by phone to Bryant, but his only demand was to be given a ride in an army helicopter. Contact was lost when the batteries in Bryant's cell phone went dead. Reinforcements arrived from Victoria and New South Wales, making this the biggest single police action in Australian history. The following morning smoke billowed from the inn and Bryant emerged, his clothes on fire. He was arrested and taken to hospital. Inside the Seascape were the bodies of the hostage and the couple who owned the inn.

Investigations revealed that Bryant was an eccentric loner. His IQ was modest, but after leaving school he worked as a handyman for a middle-aged heiress, Helen Harvey. The couple reputedly became lovers. When Harvey died in a car accident, Bryant inherited her fortune. Suggestions that Bryant caused her death were checked out, but the police cleared him. Despite his new-found wealth, he was never able to build satisfactory personal relationships. Opinions vary as to whether the killings were impulsive or planned in advance, but Bryant fits the classic profile of a spree killer: a white man, killing primarily within his own race, a drifter who had failed to achieve very much in his life and whose rampage was, if not completely unplanned, at least very difficult to predict. In murdering thirty-five people and injuring eighteen others, Bryant became Australia's worst spree killer. His crimes led to new laws regulating gun ownership, including bans on the import and sale of most military-style semi-automatic weapons.

1 Martin Bryant, the man charged with killing thirty-five people in Tasmania.
2 A victim of the shooting is taken from a helicopter in Hobart to be treated in hospital.

1

2

CELEBRITY MURDER

Barry George, accused in 2001 of the murder of British television personality Jill Dando, was obsessed with celebrities and guns. He had a history of stalking and sex attacks. Yet, at his trial, even the prosecution admitted that it was impossible to determine with any degree of certainty why he would have killed a well-liked, uncontroversial woman. Because of the absence of a clear motive, the case against him depended on the jury's assessment of circumstantial evidence.

Jill Dando was shot in April 1999: killed with a single bullet through her head as she was about to open the front door of her London home. There were no witnesses to the crime and sightings of possible culprits in the neighborhood were inconclusive. A massive murder investigation was launched, but progress was slow. Many leads proved false: for example, a man who had telephoned Dando's gas, electricity, and water suppliers pretending to be her brother proved to be a freelance journalist; and someone who checked her private address on the internet had simply made a mistake. The bullet casing had handmade indentations, but did not lead to the killer: it seems that the crimping was used to hold the 9mm bullet in the barrel of either a handgun or a previously deactivated weapon.

As other possibilities were explored only to be dismissed, the police started to focus their attention on stalkers, and the name of a man who lived near Jill Dando, Barry George, came up. First questioned almost a year after the killing, he was regarded as a low priority suspect until a search of his apartment by forensic scientists revealed a tiny speck of gunpowder residue, similar to material found in the victim's hair, in the pocket of an overcoat. but the coat was not sent to the forensic laboratory immediately; instead it was left close to where firearms and ammunition had been kept, raising the possibility of contamination. That speck, however, became vital in the case against George. Some of the many newspapers in his apartment mentioned Dando, but although he kept many photographs of women he had followed, none were of the victim. Identification evidence from people near the crime scene was also of little use to the prosecution.

George was regarded as a harmless eccentric, but closer investigation revealed a darker side. Born in London in 1960, he led a troubled life. His parents divorced and so did he. He never settled into a job and was discharged after a brief and unsuccessful stint as a private in the Territorial Army. He was a member of a gun club who impersonated famous people and his convictions included a prison sentence for attempted rape.

George did not give evidence in his own defense. His lawyer argued that the case against him was "hanging by the merest of threads," that is, the telltale speck of gunpowder residue that might conceivably have been contaminated. After deliberating for more than thirty hours, the jury found him guilty by a ten-to-one majority. The case is significant in that a conviction had been won on the basis of a trace amount of forensic evidence.

The convicted killer, Barry George.

A FISHY TALE

In July 1996, a British trawler fished up a body. It was the corpse of a man, clothed, with the pants pockets pulled out. There were no identifying marks except for a tattoo on the right hand. The man's scalp was badly gashed and he wore an expensive wristwatch—a Rolex Oyster Perpetual self-winding chronometer. Rolex traced the serial number on the watch, and gave the police an address in Essex. The police arrived to find an empty flat but were given the name of a man called Davis who had acted as a contact for the occupant, a Mr. Platt. Davis was traced but could shed no light on Platt's death. At this point no crime was suspected.

To tie up loose ends in the inquiry, the police decided to re-interview Davis. They knocked on the door of the house next to his by accident and the owner said that his neighbors were Ronald Platt and his young wife Noelle; he had never heard of Davis. The police arrested Ronald and Noelle Platt on suspicion of murder without being aware of their true identities. But as their investigations continued, an extraordinary plot began to unravel.

Platt's real name was Albert Walker. He was a Canadian financial advisor who, accompanied by his daughter Sheena, had fled to Britain in 1990 with millions of dollars of his clients' money. He met Platt, a television engineer who dreamed of emigrating to Canada, and over a period of eighteen months he gradually assumed Platt's identity and even paid for Platt and his girlfriend to go to Canada. He persuaded Platt to give him his driver's license, credit cards, and birth certificate and had rubber stamps made up with a copy of Platt's signature. Eventually, however, Platt returned to England,

penniless and disillusioned. Walker gave Platt more money, but became afraid that the existence of two Ronald Platts would lead to discovery of the truth. To preserve his false identity he needed to eliminate his alter ego. He therefore took Platt for a sail on his yacht and, when they were a few miles offshore, clubbed Platt with an anchor, pushed it through his belt, and threw him overboard.

Walker took great pains to cover his tracks, even down to removing the navigation system from the boat, which could provide evidence of where he had been. He told his daughter that Platt had left for France, packed up Platt's possessions, and put them into storage. But he had forgotten to remove Platt's Rolex and when the trawler happened to picked up Platt's body, the way was clear for conscientious detective work, aided by the luck of knocking on the wrong door, to uncover a murder that the police did not even know about.

Ronald Platt, pictured wearing the Rolex watch that eventually incriminated his murderer, Albert Walker. Right, police examine the interior of Walker's yacht where the murder took place.

DR. DEATH

The number of people whom Dr. Harold Shipman killed is not known and may never be known, but the total may be close to three hundred. The Shipman case differs from most homicide investigations in that there was no suspicion of murder. He was therefore able to continue with his serial killings, untroubled by police inquiries.

Shipman was a doctor practicing in Hyde, near Manchester, England. He was highly regarded in his community and popular with his patients. An intelligent family man, he earned the trust of people with whom he came into contact, and friends and members of his family have found it difficult to accept that he could have been a killer. His crimes came to light when the will of one of his deceased patients, a former mayor of Hyde, was produced. The patient had, apparently, disinherited her daughter and given the bulk of her estate to Shipman. Her daughter, who was a lawyer, was shocked since there had been no rift in the family. (It later emerged that Shipman had forged the will.) A local doctor then raised concerns about the high death rate among Shipman's patients: the coroner had referred those concerns to the police, but their investigations were at first inconclusive. When they probed more deeply, however, a shocking pattern came to light.

Shipman was accused of murdering fifteen elderly patients by giving them lethal doses of diamorphine. He pleaded not guilty but he was convicted in every case and received fifteen life sentences. The evidence against him was overwhelming: what was less clear was the extent of his homicidal activities. Greater Manchester Police drew up a list of twenty-one typical characteristics of a Shipman killing. Most of his victims were elderly women, usually widows or people living alone. Generally, they died at home in the afternoon, following complaints about a

minor ailment. In most cases, the victim saw Shipman on the day of death. There were striking similarities between the crime scenes: the door of the victim's house was usually open and her body would be found upright on a chair or sofa; the victim would seem to be peaceful or asleep and would be wearing her everyday clothes; Shipman would have made no physical examination of the deceased, but would inform relatives that no autopsy was required—and the cause of death pronounced by Shipman would have a weak association with the victim's clinical history.

Since Shipman has never admitted guilt, his motive remains a matter for speculation. Early in his medical career he was disciplined for misusing the drug pethidine, to which he seems to have developed an addiction. He was, however, allowed to resume his practice. Although his patients may have had minor health problems, there is no indication that these were mercy killings. The victims' ages led relatives to mistakenly accept that their deaths were from natural causes. The most likely explanation for the murders is that they allowed Shipman to play God and that he relished holding the power of life and death over his trusting and defenseless patients.

Dr. Harold Shipman's former surgery in Hyde.

A REQUEST FOR DEATH?

There was never much doubt that Marthinus Rossouw killed Baron Dieter Van Schauroth on March 24, 1961. The question that made the case celebrated was: did Van Schauroth arranged his own death?

Van Schauroth had moved from Namibia to live in a Cape Town apartment with his young wife Colleen. He came from a wealthy family but had squandered most of his money. Nevertheless, he took out large and expensive insurance policies on his own life, incurring premiums that he seemed to be unable to afford. In January 1961, he met Marthinus Rossouw, a rail worker whose associates included diggers involved in the illegal sale of diamonds. According to Rossouw, the two men became good friends, despite the difference in their backgrounds, and Van Schauroth confided that his marriage was failing. Rossouw said that the baron asked him if he would be willing to murder someone and, thinking it was a joke, Rossouw said he would.

By Rossouw's account, on March 24 they met and drove out north of Cape Town, stopping at a number of bars on the way. But Van Schauroth insisted they pretend not to know each other. Eventually, they turned onto a deserted road about twenty-four miles from the city. Van Schauroth handed his friend a gun and two boxes of cartridges. He loaded the gun, using a handkerchief, and then asked Rossouw to shoot him. Rossouw claimed to have refused, but the baron was insistent, saying that there were no witnesses and the killing could be made to look like a diamonds deal gone wrong. He said he could not kill himself, since that would mean that his wife would be unable to collect the insurance money. The baron continued to plead with a reluctant Rossouw and eventually offered money.

In the end, Rossouw shot the baron, as requested, in the back of the neck. Rossouw then returned home and threw the gun and the cartridges into the sea.

It did not take the police long to trace the connection between the baron and his murderer, who was arrested and charged with murder. The prosecution disputed Rossouw's story, maintaining that the motive for the killing was financial gain and the judge pointed out that if the marriage was unhappy, it was unlikely that the baron would go to such lengths to enrich his wife. Forensic evidence did not completely support Rossouw's claims and he kept changing details of his story. Under South African law, since Rossouw had admitted the crime, the jury was bound to find him guilty of murder, but they were entitled to find "extenuating circumstances" if appropriate: such a conclusion might save the accused from execution. Within an hour the jury returned a guilty verdict, with no extenuating circumstances, and Rossouw was duly hanged. Despite the improbability of his tale, some observers believe it to be true in its essentials. The insurance companies reached an agreement with Van Schauroth's family on the payments due under the policies that had, supposedly, constituted a motive for murder by request.

Spent cartridges, as would have been thrown into the sea by Rossouw to hide his crime.

NIGHTMARE NURSE

In 1991, Grantham and Kesteven Hospital was short staffed and suffering from the financial constraints of Britain's National Health Service. Needing to recruit nurses, management took on a twenty-three-year-old woman named Beverley Allitt. Her record of sickness absence during her nurse's training had been appalling, but few other checks were made on her background.

Within little more than seven weeks, children who were patients in Ward Four of the hospital suffered a series of ailments, injuries, and deaths. The first to die was Liam Taylor, a baby admitted with a heavy chest cold: his heart stopped beating and he died in his parents' arms. The next victim was an eleven-year-old who suffered from epilepsy but who died of a heart attack. A fifteen-month-old baby's heart stopped twice and a five-month-old, Paul Crampton, was afflicted by hypoglycemia. A sample of Paul's blood was sent for analysis, but the matter was not considered urgent and more than two weeks passed before it was discovered that the level of insulin in the blood was abnormally high. Meanwhile, a five-year-old had stopped breathing and doctors at a second hospital to which he had been transferred concluded that he had been incorrectly given a drug, which proved to be potassium. There were five more victims, two of whom died: the initial diagnoses were cot death and asthma.

The finding that Paul Crampton had apparently been injected with insulin was met with amazement at the hospital. Security was increased, but the police were not told immediately. When detectives visited the hospital they found that some pages, including those relating to the baby Paul, had been removed from the ward notebook. Questioning soon established that Beverley Allitt's presence was a common denominator in all the incidents under investigation. Her bedroom was searched and some missing medical records found. She had been injecting children with insulin or potassium and, in some cases, suffocating them.

Allitt was found guilty of four murders as well as other attacks on children in her care. She was diagnosed as suffering from Munchausen's Syndrome by Proxy, a personality disorder reflecting low self-esteem that manifests itself in an uncontrollable urge to seek attention, often by causing injury to others. Her sickness record, which was in essence a long list of imaginary ailments, was a symptom, as was the anorexia nervosa to which she succumbed following her arrest. She had a history of violence toward a former boyfriend, and dishonesty. Allitt liked to present herself as a concerned care-giver: she was trusted by her patient's parents and was even asked to become godmother to one of her victims. In truth, her crimes were attempts by an inadequate young woman to demonstrate self-worth through the exercise of power and cruelty over defenseless babies and children.

Beverley Allitt arrives at court to face accusations of the murder of several children.

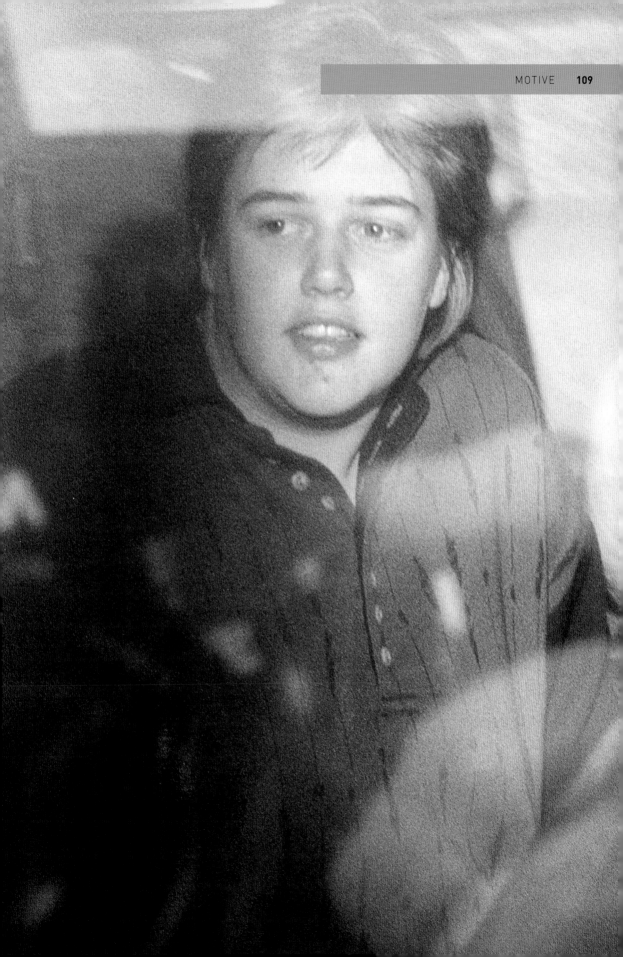

HUNGRY FOR HUMANS

Alone among killers who have indulged in cannibalism, Issei Sagawa has not only achieved freedom from captivity but also a bizarre form of celebrity status. Sagawa, an intelligent but reserved man, was born into a wealthy Japanese family in 1949. He was living in France at the time of his crime, as a graduate student doing research at the Sorbonne, in Paris. As a small boy he had participated in family games at birthday parties where "Giants and Cannibals" involved the adults pretending to put the children in a pot for cooking and eating. These games made a huge impression on him and he developed a morbid fascination with the idea of being eaten or of himself eating human flesh. A very small and unattractive man, he became obsessed with beautiful Western women and there may have been an obscure racial, as well as sexual, component in his crime.

Although he found it difficult to establish satisfactory personal relationships, he became strongly attracted to a fellow student, a twenty-five-year-old Dutch woman named Renee Hartevelt. She appears to have treated him more sympathetically than other girls in the class, although they were not lovers, and on the evening of June 11, 1981 she agreed to go with him to his apartment when he asked her for some help with a translation. Sagawa gave her tea to drink, but laced it with whisky. He then shot her in the back of the head and stripped and raped her. After dismembering her body with an electric carving knife, he proceeded to spend the next two days dining on her flesh, which he later described as "delicious," whether fried or raw. He then put Renee's remains into two suitcases and threw them into a pool in the Bois de Boulogne. A couple of passersby saw him and he fled. A taxi driver recalled taking Sagawa and the suitcases to the scene and the murderer was soon arrested. He confessed at once.

The judge hearing the case ruled that Sagawa was insane and he was sent to a mental hospital, but was repatriated to Japan in 1984, and won his release a mere fifteen months later. Sagawa had already been the subject of a novel written by a well-known Japanese author and had written a book of his own, *In The Fog*, which despite (or because of) its graphic descriptions of what he had done to Renee, became a bestseller. He continued to write and paint successfully and made guest appearances on television as well as presenting a seminar in 1994 that featured an erotic film called *The Desire to be Eaten*.

1 Issei Sagawa photographed just outside Tokyo following his release.
2 Sagawa arrives in Tokyo having been released by French authorities to receive psychiatric treatment in Japan.

CHAPTER FOUR

SOLVING MURDERS

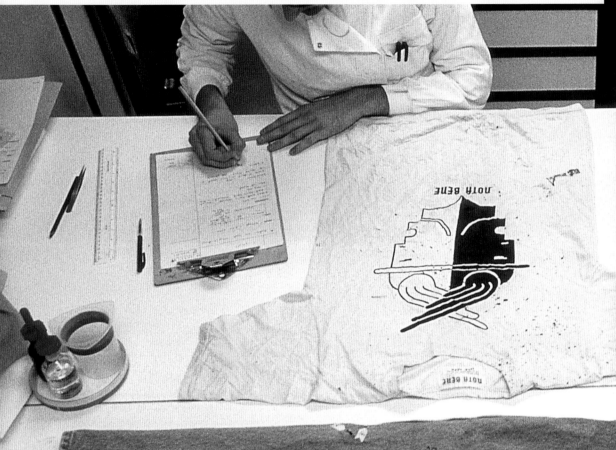

**"From any crime to its author there is a trail
... And finding and following such trails is
what a detective is paid to do."**

Dashiell Hammett, *Dead Yellow Woman* (1947)

Murder investigations are inevitably complex. They are also infinitely variable. Planning an investigation demands not only organizational skills and sound judgment, but also a degree of flexibility and a capacity for lateral thinking.

Although mundane, the question of resources cannot be ignored by those in charge of the investigation. Neither can it be overlooked by a writer seeking to deal thoroughly with the issues that need to be addressed in real life. A murder investigation is resource-intensive, and while inappropriate cost-cuttings should not be made, a decision must be made at the outset as to how large the investigating team should be and how best to utilize the people and facilities available.

Rapid decisions need to be made in any murder case, but even where time pressure is acute, it is vital to think those decisions through. It is a good idea to record the decisions and why they were made. This is not mere bureaucracy: decisions made, even in the heat of the moment, may later be scrutinized at great length in court proceedings. A good record will also help in the evaluation of investigative decisions, which may happen months or even years later. It is sensible to try to anticipate criticisms that may be made, and to pre-empt them

Crime scene investigators in the Bronx, New York, collecting and photographing everything before removal for forensic examination.

Previous page: Forensic scientists examine clothing and shoes of a murder victim and take samples of blood from them for testing.

by outlining a justification of the decision-making process that will stand up to scrutiny. A variety of strategies may be relevant to the investigation and it is important to set these on the record. A realistic crime novel should not be over-burdened by bureaucratic details, but nor should it ignore the practical importance of those details to the detectives.

Determining a suitable forensic strategy is a priority, since crime scenes are precious and frequently yield evidence that leads to the conviction of the offender. Careful management of the scene is therefore vital and this usually involves taking a "forensic overview" before an attempt is made to assess the scene in detail. Forensic intelligence plays a key part in a murder investigation, although by itself it often does not provide sufficient proof of guilt.

ASSESSING THE CRIME SCENE

Crime scenes are often important in fiction because of the atmosphere that their authentic portrayal may add to the story, but their significance goes far beyond that. In addition to forensic evidence found there, the crime scene may also yield information about the offender. For example, where a murderer has committed the crime at one place and then moved the body to another, questions will arise about the distance between the scene of the murder and the site where the body was found. Often, the distance between the two locations is short, although it is greater in the case of a child victim: the weight and age of the victim often have a bearing on how far the corpse has been moved. Movement of the body may provide further clues about the physical capabilities of the offender. In abduction cases there are usually three relevant scenes: that of the abduction; the place of death; and the location of the body. Sometimes the first two scenes are never discovered, but research suggests that the abduction site tends to be more closely related to the offender's home and daily routine than the site where the body is left.

Investigators need to consider why or how the crime scene was chosen by the offender. It may have been an entirely random choice. Or, it may have been selected for a reason relevant to the victim, the offender, or both such as familiarity of location. The means by which the victim and offender arrived at the scene, and by which the offender left it, may also be important: for example witness sightings of a vehicle or vehicles, coming to or leaving the scene.

Forensic evidence may clarify the nature of the encounter between the victim and the culprit. The victim may, for instance, have been induced or compelled to go to a certain location. The evidence might suggest that they met by chance, or that the offender selected the location for attack in the belief that there was little or no danger of being disturbed or discovered there.

Finally, the location must be viewed in context. The surrounding environment, whether urban or rural, may provide important evidence, including information about connections between the scene and the victim or attacker. Senior investigative officers frequently inspect the scene itself, even if the hunt for forensic evidence is left to others on the team, since the context of the scene cannot be fully understood by viewing photographs or video footage alone.

VICTIMOLOGY

In the vast majority of murder cases there is some form of connection between the perpetrator and the victim. Investigators need to focus on victimology, that is, an overall assessment of the victim's circumstances with an eye toward ascertaining the reason for the crime and drawing up a list of potential suspects. Such assessments offer the crime writer endless plot possibilities, as well as raw material for character development.

The reason the victim was at the crime scene needs to be as fully understood as possible. His or her presence may be explained by work or social activities; if not, another viable reason needs to be identified. Or there may be a link between the victim and someone at or near the scene.

The victim's past provides crucial data in many cases. If he or she has been prey to the attentions of a stalker, for instance, that will suggest an immediate line of inquiry. It may be that the victim's lifestyle or personal habits are significant, for example where the victim was a prostitute, known criminal, or police informant. The victim's job or leisure activities may also be relevant, and the same is true of places that he or she was known to have frequented, such as bars or casinos. The victim's family background is central to many murder inquiries and the nature of his or her personal relationships with others is often highly significant. It is worth looking at the reactions of close family members to news of the murder to see whether they yield any telltale signs of guilt. At the same time, too much should not be read into an apparently emotionless reaction. The same can be said for a "bereaved" person who appears to be very upset by the crime—such as Jeremy Bamber, convicted of killing five family members and staging the scene to suggest that his sister was responsible.

Finally, the victim's personal characteristics deserve analysis. A notably aggressive—or timid—personality may well offer clues to the crime. If the victim had a disability or was vulnerable in some other way, that too may be relevant. Explorations of character and motive are central to true-life crimes as well as the best crime novels.

ASSESSING THE OFFENDER

The MO employed by the offender supplies clues to the investigating team that will be helpful when the time comes to draw up a psychological profile of the culprit. A range of factors may influence the choice of MO, such as:

- childhood background (such as a history of physical or sexual abuse)
- mental state
- education or training (a suspect's training as a butcher or surgeon may be relevant in dismemberment cases)
- history of offending
- opportunity

An offender who is not mentally unstable will try to choose an MO that enables him to commit the crime successfully and avoid detection. The offender's previous history may contribute to the MO used in a particular crime. Aspects of the MO, such as choice of location, will be geared to particular circumstances. Geographical profiling may also prove helpful: this is a concept pioneered in Canada by Kim Rossmo, and involves the analysis of evidence with a view toward determining the likely home or workplace of the offender. Geographical profiling is especially useful in the case of serial killings.

Other aspects of the MO may reflect a kind of ritual practiced by the offender. This is described as the offender's signature. Investigators may be able to conclude whether the culprit seems to have acted alone or with one or more accomplices. In some cases the crime scene is disguised or arranged, perhaps to conceal the corpse from view or to display a signature, as with the crimes of Albert DeSalvo, the Boston Strangler. Investigators assess the level of risk that the offender took in committing the crime at the scene and whether, for example, an escape route had been planned in advance. Other factors that contribute toward the overall picture include any attempts by the offender to exert physical control over the victim and the length of time (if it can be determined) that the offender spent with the victim while committing the crime.

In the late 1970s, profilers such as Robert K. Ressler at the FBI's Behavioral Sciences Unit at Quantico coined the distinction between organized and disorganized crime scenes and offenders. Of course, it is a very broad distinction and some scenes and some killers display a mix of both characteristics. But the dichotomy has still provided investigators with a useful analytical tool with which to look at four phases of the crime:

- the pre-crime stage
- the commission of the crime
- the disposal of the body
- post-crime behavior

The essence of the organized offender is premeditation, coupled with planning. In the case of serial killers, planning usually flows from their fantasies, typically of a violent or sexual nature. Organized offenders target victims who fit a particular profile: for example, Son of Sam, David Berkowitz, sought out women who were either alone or with a man in a parked car. The organized offender may use trickery to gain control of the victim: John Wayne Gacy offered cash to young men to go back to his house to perform sex acts.

Disorganized offenders, in contrast, lack method and interest in their victims as people; hence their tendency to hide or disfigure their victims' faces. They do not develop increasing expertise in murder techniques or take trophies from their victims. Their personalities are, generally, very different from those of organized offenders: they will, for the most part, have internalized their rage and under-achieved in life. Conversely, organized offenders may, at least on the surface, be attractive and charming, although it is rare for them to sustain successful long-term relationships: the serial killer Ted Bundy is just one example.

PROCESS AT THE CRIME SCENE

Homicide detection, perhaps more than any other form of crime detection, begins with proper procedure at the scene of crime. It is no exaggeration to say that a successful outcome to a homicide investigation may depend upon the first officer responding being able to properly identify, isolate, and secure the scene. It is vital to restrict access to the scene to authorized personnel only and to make sure that evidence is not destroyed. A

1 Comforted by his girlfriend Julie Mugford, Jeremy Bamber leaves his family's funeral looking distressed (see page 117).
2 The FBI Behavioral Science Unit in Quantico.
3 Forensic scientists remove the body of a murder victim: the nature of death can lead detectives directly to a suspect, particularly if they have offended before in a similar way.

THEN AND NOW

DNA PROFILING

The most remarkable forensic detection technique of all is DNA profiling, also known as genetic fingerprinting. Deoxyribonucleic acid, or DNA, is the genetic material of the cell. Our physical characteristics are to a large extent determined by our DNA. Certain structures of DNA are more or less unique to a particular person. No one else will have the same DNA on those particular structures, unless he or she has an identical twin. A sample of human tissue will provide a source of DNA.

The potential of DNA profiling was discovered in 1984 by Alec (now Sir Alec) Jeffreys, a British academic. While conducting medical research, Jeffreys found a way of showing the genetic variations between different people on X-ray film. After using enzymes to cut up the DNA, Jeffreys discovered a method of measuring the different pieces. In this process, the cut DNA is placed in a slab of gel, and an electric current then pushes the DNA through the gel. The shorter the piece of DNA, the further it travels. The resulting pattern of bands provides the unique genetic profile.

The technique was first applied to homicide investigation in a 1987 case in Leicestershire, England, as part of the investigation of the rape and murder of two teenage girls. A mass blood-sampling exercise of men in the area at first yielded no results. It then developed that a local bakery worker, Colin Pitchfork, had persuaded a colleague to submit a blood sample posing as Pitchfork. Pitchfork's subsequent confession and conviction marked DNA profiling as a forensic breakthrough, news of which rapidly traveled throughout the world.

Questions inevitably emerged about the reliability of the new technique. Within a year of the British case, an American homicide investigation saw DNA testing itself on trial. Judge Gerald Sheindlin ruled that DNA profiling is scientifically capable of distinguishing one individual from another, even though on the actual facts of the case before him, because the DNA test had not been properly performed, the facts could not be submitted to a jury. In an extraordinary twist, the defendant, Joseph Castro, changed his plea to guilty in return for a plea bargain and made admissions indicating that the prosecution's case on the DNA match had, despite the flaws in the process been well founded. The Castro case led to the establishment of a series of standards that laboratories generally adhere to today, and a drive to make DNA profiling techniques more consistently reliable.

Analyzing small samples of DNA was problematic from the outset. It was only overcome by the development in the U.S. of a new technique of analysis. This is Polymires Chain Reaction (PCR). DNA from the sample is split by heating and polymires enzymes are then added to make copies of selected DNA fragments. These vary in size between different people. Each copy process is repeated over and over again to produce a chain reaction that yields almost unlimited amounts of DNA. This means that even the smallest amounts of DNA can be tested and re-tested.

As the technology has developed, so has demand increased in many countries for the establishment of a criminal DNA database. Profiles may be entered into such a database after the very first offense. Because of PCR technology, which expresses DNA profiles in numbers rather than in bands on X-ray

A magnifying glass shows an example of a DNA
fingerprint, arranged in four rows of irregularly
spaced black bands that make up the genetic code
which is unique to every person.

plates, computers can rapidly compare the sample with DNA collected at thousands of crime scenes.
Currently, the largest such database is in Birmingham, England. Following legislation in 1994, it has
become a storage facility for over one hundred thousand DNA samples found at crime scenes. It also
includes DNA from over one million people who have either committed a crime or are being investigated.
Any new DNA received is automatically checked by computer to see whether it matches the DNA from
another crime scene. But this brings up the question of what is deemed to be a match. The early six-point
comparison generated occasional coincidental matches (even at very long odds) and has now been
superseded by a ten-point matching standard.

rope or barrier usually defines the perimeter of the scene, excluding unauthorized access. Best practice generally requires a three-tiered perimeter: the outer perimeter excludes onlookers and other unauthorized personnel; an inner perimeter allows for a command post outside the crime scene; and the scene itself is subject to minimum access, even for authorized personnel.

The process of evidence gathering begins from the moment the first officer arrives. An immediate task is to record transient details, for example any relevant weather conditions or items on the scene displaced by a doctor attending the corpse. Much evidence is fragile and needs to be bagged immediately before it is lost or damaged. But the task must not be rushed; mistakes made in haste may be impossible to fix.

A key source of information is witnesses at or near the scene. Initial descriptions need to be made of everyone at the location, bearing in mind that it is common for killers to remain at or return to the scene.

Teamwork is crucial. The team leader, on arrival, takes control of the scene and assumes responsibility for the safety of personnel and the security of the area. The team leader also makes an initial survey of the scene, evaluating possible evidence and preparing a description of it. He or she is responsible for assigning tasks to members of the team and co-operating as appropriate with other law enforcement agencies.

A vital member of the team is the photographer, who should photograph the scene before it is extensively accessed, and perhaps disrupted, by colleagues. A single photograph is not enough: overall, middle-range, and close-up shots are necessary, as are accurate measurement scales. Significant items of evidence need to be recorded photographically before being moved, including latent fingerprints and other impression evidence, which is eventually lifted in cast. A log of the photographs is then compiled by a photographic log recorder. Videotaping the scene can also be very helpful—not the least as a good way to familiarize and brief the team later.

A sketch artist usually records the immediate scene and significant items of evidence, noting and checking any relevant measurements. If the sketch is not drawn to scale, that fact should be made clear.

The evidence recorder has to describe each item of evidence and the place where it was found on the appropriate container, usually a bag or envelope. Liquids are best preserved in leak-proof, unbreakable containers. There is a great need to avoid contamination of the evidence, so any items that might cross-contaminate each other must be kept in separate packages. The evidence container must be signed and dated. It is crucial to maintain the "chain of custody" and avoid any contamination of evidence that could jeopardize prosecution later. A log of these items is maintained to keep track of the material.

The team includes a wide range of specialists. Each specialist needs to be competent in his or her field and have an appreciation of the nature of a homicide investigation. Furthermore, since the specialist may have to give evidence once the perpetrator has been identified, it is important for that specialist to have the experience and ability to present compelling testimony in court without being overly vulnerable to hostile cross-examination.

Specialists who may be called upon include experts in the following fields:

- anthropology
- blood pattern analysis
- engineering
- entomology
- odontology
- psychological profiling

In recent years, crime novels have focused increasingly on the role of the psychological profiler. Val McDermid's *The Mermaids Singing* (1995) and *The Wire In the Blood* (1997) are good examples, while *Killing The Shadows* (2000) takes the process a step further with the serial murder of authors whose work features such profilers. There is room for exploration of the roles of other specialists: Aaron Elkins' novels follow the forensic anthropologist Gideon Oliver; Patricia D. Cornwell features the medical examiner Kay Scarpetta; and Kathy Reichs writes about the forensic anthropologist Temperance Brennan.

When the crime scene has been thoroughly documented and the evidence logged, the scene can be cleared. The priority is to collect any evidence that is most likely to get lost, damaged, or destroyed. Removing one item of evidence may reveal another that has previously been unnoticed, so the recording process may not yet be completed.

PSYCHOLOGICAL PROFILING

Psychological profiling has become increasingly important in homicide investigations. It is now widely accepted that criminals tend to leave evidence of their motivations—perhaps traces of their distinctive characteristics—at a crime scene. Psychological profiling makes use of the behavioral scientist, the psychologist, and the psychiatrist to analyze this type of evidence.

Criminal profiling and offender profiling are terms commonly used, but psychological profiling may refer to both the victim and the criminal. Experts have developed the concept of the psychological autopsy, that is, a profile of the deceased person. This can help cast light on whether, for instance, someone who appears to have been a victim of murder in fact committed suicide.

Profiling has hit the headlines in recent years, particularly following the success of Thomas Harris's novel *The Silence of the Lambs* (1988) and the Oscar-winning film based on it. The best profilers are acutely aware of the uniqueness of each individual. An ability to assess what is consistent about a person from one set of circumstances to another is one of the profiler's main tools. In looking at the various ways in which individuals relate to each other, profilers are likely to look at the extent to which a perpetrator tries to relate to his or her victim and to what extent there is evidence of a desire to dominate them. The British profiler David Canter acknowledges in his book *Criminal Shadows* (1994) that "a crucial part of reading the shadows a criminal casts is to be able to recognise which are his shadows and which are those of another, possibly similar offender." Unfortunately, this is easier said than done. There are dangers in relying too heavily on psychological

1 Police recover an axe from a pond on Wimbledon Common in London in connection with the murder of Rachel Nickell in 1995.
2 A still from the film *Silence of the Lambs*.
3 A hair sample from a suspect is prepared for analysis in a forensic laboratory.
4 The scene of the murder of Sharon Tate.
5 Blood group testing of blood stained clothing.

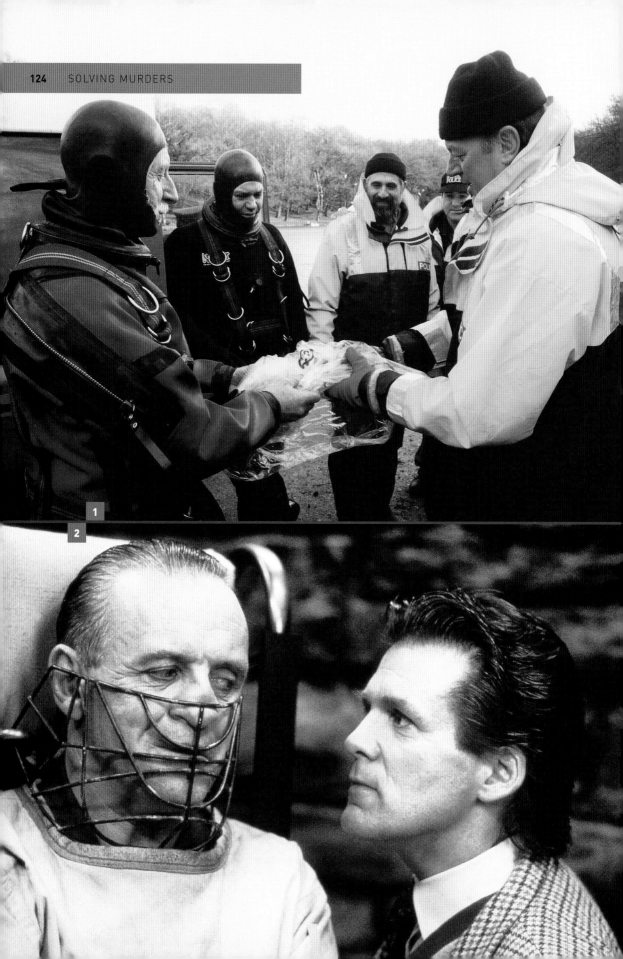

profiling on its own. The homicide investigation team needs, for instance when seeking to link together crimes that appear to form a series, to focus on hard forensic evidence as well, in seeking to build a picture of the likely offender.

John Douglas has described in *Journey Into Darkness* (1997, written with Mark Olshaker) the belief of the profilers at Quantico that "behavior reflects personality" and a seven-phase approach to the profiling process, as follows:

- evaluating the criminal act
- evaluating the specifics of the crime scene
- analyzing the victim
- evaluating preliminary police reports
- evaluating the medical examiner's autopsy protocol
- developing a profile with "critical offender characteristics"
- making suggestions for the investigation on the basis of the profile

The next step is to suggest ideas to the investigating team for getting the culprit to "make a move." This may even go so far as suggesting that a decoy be used as bait to tempt the culprit to repeat the crime. But this is risky. The British criminologist Brian Masters wrote a powerful essay, "Evidence of Entrapment," about the failure of profiling in the unsuccessful prosecution of Colin Stagg for the murder of Rachel Nickell in London, in 1992. He suggested that profiling sometimes places too much weight on hunches, which can often be unsupported.

An important element of the profiler's work in some homicide cases may be to identify the killer's signature or psychological calling card, left at each crime scene in cases of serial murder. The killer's signature is not the same as his or her MO:

the latter is the way in which the crimes are committed—at a particular time of day, in a particular location, or with particular tools. But many killers feel a need to go beyond their MO and leave a special imprint or signature at the scene. Robert D. Keppel, a veteran crime investigator and expert in signature crimes, argues in *Signature Killers* (1997, written with William J. Birnes) that "the core of the killer's imprint will never change," although he agrees with the FBI's behavioral scientists' view that the signature elements may become more fully developed as the killer gains in confidence. The calling card may be how the criminal chooses or controls the victim, or disposes of the corpse. Again, determining the signature demands careful examination of the crime scene—and often an understanding of the victim's psychological profile.

Profiling becomes ever more sophisticated. VICAP (the Violent Criminal Apprehension Program) was introduced at Quantico in 1985. Homicides often generate hundreds or even thousands of potential suspects. Profilers making efficient use of computers can help the investigating team to narrow the search to a relatively small group of principal suspects. But before a solution can be found a great deal of work must be done, quickly but carefully.

FORENSIC INFORMATION FROM THE SCENE AND THE AUTOPSY

Interpreting forensic evidence is critical. Initial questions include:

- how does forensic evidence gathered at the scene help identify the victim and the offender?
- is there evidence to indicate that the crime had a sexual component?

> does the evidence suggest that the offender was "forensically aware" (that is, has the offender destroyed potentially incriminating evidence, or worn gloves or used a condom)?
>
> has physical evidence been left by the offender?
>
> has anything been removed from the crime scene?
>
> what information is provided by blood at the scene?
>
> is there evidence to link the scene with either the victim or the offender?

TYPES OF EVIDENCE

A crime scene will often, though not always, provide various kinds of physical evidence, some of which may be crucial to conviction of the offender. Finding the murder weapon is an obvious priority, but once the weapon or any other significant evidence is obtained, its significance needs to be fully understood. In the Sharon Tate murder case in 1969, a distinctive gun, missing its right-hand grip, was found; but then it was simply tagged and filed away in a manila envelope. Not for some time was its importance fully recognized; eventually it provided a crucial link to the culprit, Charles Manson, and his "family" of followers.

In many murder cases, DNA evidence is crucial. Various forms of DNA profiling techniques are available and even though detectives are not expected to be experts in forensic science, they need to have an understanding of the potential of those techniques for their investigations. For example, there is a specialized form of DNA profiling called Mitochondrial DNA (Mt DNA) profiling that can be very valuable. Mt DNA is found in the contents of every cell, rather than in the nucleus of the cell. It is inherited only through the mother and therefore cannot provide results as precise as certain other forms of DNA profiling. However, since it is present throughout every cell, including a hair cell, investigators may be able to take advantage of the fact that hair is often found at crime scenes.

Blood is also frequently found at crime scenes. DNA profiling of blood at the scene may help identify both the victim and the murderer. The pattern of blood stains found at the scene often provides important information about the sequence of events in a fight or physical attack. Bloodstains on clothing may also help to prove a connection between the wearer and the murderer. Even if bloodstains are not apparent to the naked eye, it is good procedure to send key items of evidence for expert examination where sensitive chemical techniques and low-power microscopy can reveal otherwise invisible traces of blood. The analysis of bloodstains and blood patterns is a highly specialized task that of necessity involves a degree of subjective judgment, making it imperative that the specialist is given any information about the crime that may influence the conclusions he or she may draw from the blood evidence.

Given the rapid developments in, and enormous importance of, DNA testing, any blood or body fluid is likely to provide important evidence that needs to be carefully preserved. Even a minute fragment of DNA may prove crucial in determining the guilt—or innocence—of a suspect. Samples should be preserved, even if it appears that the amount of DNA available is so small that matching it to a suspect is impossible using current techniques: there has been an

THE LIE DETECTOR

Even the most experienced homicide investigators may find it difficult to decide whether a suspect is telling the truth. So it is not surprising that, for over a century, there has been a search for scientific equipment that will help determine whether or not a person is telling the truth. In 1895 the Italian Cesare Lombroso adapted the medical instruments plethysmograph and sphygmograph to produce a forerunner of the modern lie detector. The suspect had to wear an airtight volumetric glove that was attached to a rubber membrane and activated a pen that rolled over the surface of a smoked drum, varying with the subject's blood flow. The idea was that when a person tells a lie, the stress of deception affects his or her heart rate and blood pressure and by observing the deviations traced by the pen, an investigator would see when the subject was lying.

William Marston pioneered the modern lie detector—a machine he devised toward the end of World War I that he said could detect verbal deception by measuring an increase in systolic blood pressure. But in 1923, a federal circuit court upheld a murder conviction in the case of Frye v. United States even though the defendant appealed on the basis that testimony from an examiner about a systolic blood pressure deception test that he had passed was not accepted as evidence. The court ruled that such expert evidence would only be admitted if it had gained general acceptance. In other words, pioneering or experimental evidence would carry little or no weight until the fundamentals upon which it was based were accepted by the consensus of expert opinion. Such a consensus has, with lie detectors, been slow in coming. Bruno Hauptmann, convicted of kidnaping the baby of the aviator Charles Lindbergh, was denied his request to take a lie-detector test. He was sent to the electric chair in 1936.

Over the years, efforts were made to improve and demonstrate the reliability of polygraphs. A police officer, John Larson, constructed a machine that simultaneously measured pulse rate, blood pressure, and respiratory changes; he also developed an interviewing technique called the R/I (relevant/irrelevant) procedure. Questions relevant to the crime would be mixed in with others that were irrelevant, on the theory that an innocent subject would have a similar physiological response to both types of question, but a culprit would react more keenly to those questions that focused on the crime.

The modern polygraph is compact: a blood pressure cuff is put on the subject's arm and small metal plates attached to the fingers, while rubber tubes are positioned on his or her chest and abdomen. A moving paper feeder is employed, together with styluses that record input from skin response, relative blood pressure, and respiration. The moment when a question is asked is marked on the paper just before the response is recorded. The information recorded is interpreted by a numerical scoring system.

Supporters of the polygraph claim that its results are potentially very accurate. But opponents argue that the principles upon which the polygraph is based are seriously flawed. Just as an experienced detective may be misled by a nervous person's reaction to questioning, so a polygraph may fail to take into account the real reasons for those reactions. Publicity has been given to techniques that supposedly enable a person

Robert Manley, an associate of the murdered Elizabeth Short, was given a lie-detector test at Los Angeles, California in 1947. The test proved inconclusive.

to lie and yet still pass the polygraph test. Given the uncertainties, it is not surprising that despite apparently considerable improvements in the technology, courts still often refuse to accept the validity of lie-detector tests.

increasing number of cases where DNA samples, retained from unsolved murders of the past, have been effectively analyzed following improvements in the technology. So it is essential that DNA samples not be disposed of or contaminated in any way.

Fingerprints and palm prints are strong evidence of the presence of a person at the crime scene. Collecting prints at the scene is a priority, and non-movable prints need to be processed without delay. Prints from the victim are likely to be required for elimination purposes and fingerprints from any suspect will need to be taken promptly to enable comparisons to be made.

Bite marks are often found in cases involving a sexual attack. They should be photographed, preferably in a variety of conditions. The expert assistance of a forensic odontologist will prove invaluable here. Broken fingernails found at the scene should be kept in a paper container, as it may be possible to match a fragment of nail to the person from whom it came.

Any relevant documents found at the scene should be fingerprinted and kept in an appropriate paper container. If handwritten, the document may be matched to the person who wrote it by a handwriting expert.

Bullets and casings found at the scene can be matched to a gun in the possession of a suspect. Often, ballistics experts can identify the make and model of weapon that fired the casing or bullet; casings and bullets found at the scene should be kept in separate packages.

Shoeprints and tire tracks provide further links to a particular suspect. The prints or tracks should be photographed before collection. There are various ways of enhancing marks and features that are not clearly visible. Shoes can be linked to an individual not only by DNA but also by toe pressure marks inside them.

Fibers are often fragile and easily mislaid, damaged, or lost. They should be collected with great care as they may provide a vital match to the clothes, vehicle, or police sketch of a suspect. The best evidence, based on the principle that most fabrics transfer fibers on contact with other items, comes from the transfer of multiple fibers rather than a single fiber. The context in which fibers are found is also crucial to their interpretation, with contamination always a potential risk. The examination of textile fibers is often far from conclusive and scientists are currently unable to carry out fiber analysis on very pale clothing or material that comes into the hands of the police too long after the event. Generally, artificial fibers are easier to compare than natural ones because they are a more homogeneous, consistent product.

Other physical evidence that may be found at the scene, including glass, dust, and paint must also be preserved and recorded meticulously. However, it is one thing to suggest guidelines, another to follow them scrupulously in each and every case. A crime scene is, almost by definition, a chaotic place. It is easy to say that evidence must not be contaminated, but in the real world contamination all too easily does occur.

THE AUTOPSY

The autopsy, or post mortem, provides vital data for the investigating officers and they need to be represented when it takes place. The information

Investigators in Los Angeles collect evidence from the shooting of a German couple hiking in the mountains. The woman was killed and the man critically wounded.

to be gleaned often includes some or all of the following:

- the cause of death
- the means by which death occurred
- the manner of death (suicide, accident, homicide, or natural causes)
- how long the victim survived after the fatal attack took place
- whether the body was moved after death
- the relative positions of murderer and victim at the time of the killing
- whether there was a sexual assault on the victim
- whether the victim was sedated

Sometimes an autopsy may be carried out following exhumation of a body, for example if suspicion about the cause of death has been aroused. Autopsy scenes often feature in crime novels and the work of Patricia D. Cornwell and Kathy Reichs has achieved a new level of authenticity in the description of autopsy and related processes. Reichs is herself a noted forensic anthropologist and *Death Du Jour* (1999) opens with a gripping account of an exhumation in wintry Montreal. Cornwell spent time working as a computer analyst in the chief medical examiner's office in Virginia. Writers who lack such professional expertise would benefit from talking to pathologists in order to obtain a first-hand

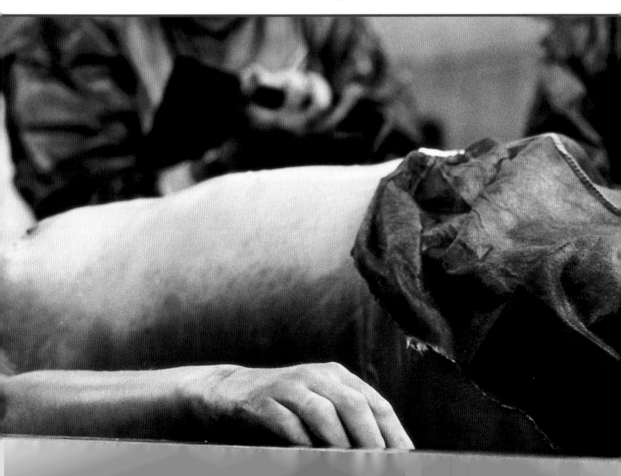

impression of the scene at a typical autopsy.

Initial details from the autopsy include:

- the cause of death
- the estimated time of death
- toxicological evidence
- the scale of force used in committing the crime
- analysis of the injuries
- any attempt by the offender to disguise the cause of death
- information about the weapon used

Mortuary technicians with the corpse of a twenty-year-old woman during an autopsy examination.

ANTICIPATING THE FUTURE

An efficient homicide investigator will try to anticipate future developments in the case, both short- and long-term. A foreseeable danger is that, when a case comes to court, the defense team will want to mount an attack on police procedure. Juries are more easily swayed by red herrings than judges and are less inclined to accept police evidence today than in days gone by. A classic defense against forensic evidence based on fibers or other items found at the crime scene is that the material was planted. This underlines the need for scrupulous care in recording evidence. The prosecution case needs to be as airtight as possible.

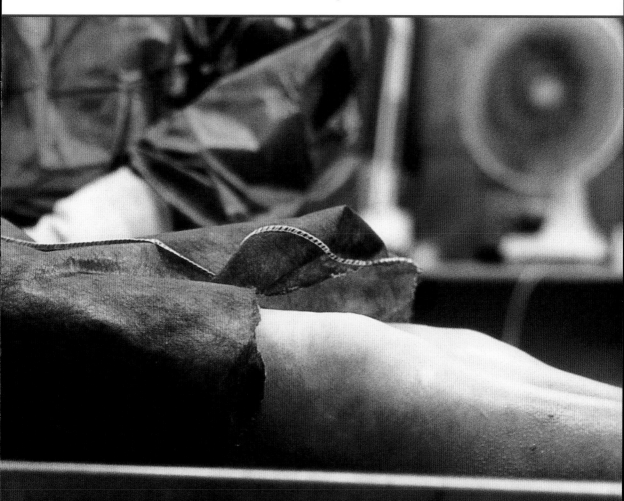

A number of cold cases—cases not solved right away—have eventually resulted in a conviction because the detectives were careful to preserve minute particles of evidence, even though the forensic science techniques available at the time did not enable those particles to be analyzed. Laboratory methods are improving all the time and advances in DNA technology have enabled justice to finally be done in many previously unsolved cases. DNA profiling can result in the dramatic reinterpretation of old crimes: the A6 murder in Britain in 1961 is a case in point. James Hanratty was hanged for shooting Michael Gregsten and injuring his lover Valerie Storie. There had long been considerable doubt about the strength of the prosecution evidence and many argued that Hanratty's execution was a serious miscarriage of justice. DNA evidence that finally became available almost forty years after the murder, however, suggested that Hanratty was guilty after all. A match was confirmed between sperm and cells left at the murder scene on a handkerchief and underwear, and samples of DNA taken from Hanratty's family. But lawyers representing the Hanratty family have argued that the DNA may have been contaminated or inaccurately interpreted and does not conclusively establish that Hanratty was the gunman. In contrast, Kenneth Waters walked free from a Massachusetts prison after serving almost twenty years for a crime he did not commit. He was convicted of the 1980 murder of Katharina Brow, but DNA evidence finally cleared him.

The validity of seemingly unequivocal confessions of guilt is also open to challenge in many cases. This underlines the need to comply with legal rules on obtaining a confession. Entrapment, for instance, may render a confession inadmissible and destroy an apparently powerful prosecution case. This happened with a confession to the murder of Rachel Nickell, made in 1993 by Colin Stagg. The confession was made to an undercover woman police officer who, acting on the advice of an eminent British psychological profiler, encouraged Stagg to explore his sexual fantasies. The judge condemned the methods used and threw out the case against Stagg. The murder remains unsolved. Investigators need to keep in close touch with expert criminal lawyers on all sensitive issues of this kind and to follow the legal guidance offered.

TIME OF DEATH

There is often doubt as to when a homicide occurred. Determining the time of death is important in establishing whether apparent alibis are valid or not. But establishing time of death is as much an art as it is a science. There are so many variables that the distinguished U.K. pathologist, Bernard Knight, has quoted his equally respected predecessor, Dr. Francis Camps, as saying, "The only way to tell the time of death is to be there when it happens!" While this may sound cynical, the reality is that homicide investigators are simply seeking what Knight describes as "a bracket of probability," which may be many hours wide. While a variety of techniques assist investigators in estimating the time of death, they need to be employed carefully and with a keen awareness of the potential margin of error.

Following death the body begins to cool, and at room temperature a corpse will typically cool at approximately 2°F (1.5°C) per hour during the first six hours following death. The rate of cooling then slows and the body usually feels cold to the touch after half a day. After a full day, body temperature is usually the same as that of the surrounding air. Therefore, if one assumes a normal living temperature of 98.6°F (37°C), temperature may point to timing. But rectal temperature is higher than normal body temperature and in any event the original body temperature may itself vary from the norm: an injured person may become hypothermic. A body placed near a source of heat may rise in temperature following death. The following factors may also affect the calculation:

clothing
amount of body fat
violent physical exertion prior to death
posture affecting heat loss
dehydration
wet or damp clothing or body surfaces
humidity

It is sometimes said that strangulation raises the temperature, but any violent struggle can have this effect. Two German academics, Henssge and Madea, have devised a computer program and a nomogram (a graph where lines are drawn across a pre-printed template) which, with the best data available, claims ninety-five percent accuracy within a time frame of plus or minus 2.3 hours. But even this system, with its substantial margin for error, is hardly infallible, since the assessment of certain variables is subjective.

Other ways of establishing the time of death are even less reliable. Rigor mortis is very unpredictable: the muscles of the corpse stiffen due to chemical changes in the body, beginning in the face and followed by the shoulders, arms, and legs. In an ordinary case, rigor may be detectable between two to four hours, firm by six to twelve hours and then continue for a day or two before

fading. Even if two people are killed at the same time, in the same place, their bodies may show significant differences in terms of rigor mortis. Electrocution can speed up rigor, as can immersion in hot water. Conversely, a corpse left outside in cold weather may experience a week's delay in rigor.

A similar phenomenon of little use to the homicide investigator is cadaveric spasm, or instantaneous rigor. This is familiar from (usually rather old-fashioned) crime novels where the corpse grips a weapon or document in the hand. But in reality, cadaveric spasm is very rare.

Post-mortem lividity or hypostasis is the settling of the blood in the lower parts of a corpse. Lividity is found in underlying parts of the body that are not in contact with a hard surface or restricted by pressure from clothing. But lividity offers few worthwhile clues about the time of death, again because there are so many variable factors such as the amount of body fat and blood loss. The coloration itself can provide some information for investigators: lividity is likely to be cherry-pink in a carbon monoxide poisoning case, brick-red in some cases of poisoning by cyanide, and brownish if the deceased has ingested certain drugs.

Stomach contents are equally unreliable as a guide to time of death. The view held in the past, that the quantity and state of digestion is fairly constant with time, has been exposed as mistaken. A very rough average emptying time may be said to be between two and four hours, but the rate and state of digestion depends on the nature and quantity of the food, especially the amounts of carbohydrate and fat and the amount of liquid consumed. Any significant physical or emotional event can slow emptying and digestion: after a head injury, digestion may stop completely. Stomach contents may, however, provide useful information if they can be linked to a particular meal taken by the deceased and it may be deduced that death occurred following that meal but before the next one was taken.

Forensic entomology provides another valuable source of information; a corpse is attractive to other forms of life. Flies tend to arrive first. A body left above ground in warm conditions will attract bluebottles and greenbottles. Insects lay their eggs in bodily orifices and the maggots that hatch in due course feed on muscle tissue. As the maggots feed and grow they shed their skins until they have absorbed sufficient nutrients to be able to burrow in the soil and pupate. The outer skin hardens and contracts forming a pupal case. In time, the adult fly emerges from the case and the cycle begins again. The value of studying maggots is that they may help determine how much time has passed since death. Even though it will be unknown when the fly reached the corpse, determining how long the maggot has been alive can indicate the shortest period of time that has elapsed since death.

There may be other clues as to the time of death through decomposition of a body buried in the ground without the benefit of a coffin.

1 A surgeon holds a vial containing maggots that can give valuable information on the date of death of a corpse.
2 Bones from the dismembered body of Colonel Percy Fawcett in 1951.
3 The skull of the murdered Mrs Ruxton superimposed over a photograph of her to confirm the identity of the skull.
4 A reconstruction of the face of a young man whose skeleton was found on a Wythall rubbish dump in London in 1991.
5 A reconstruction of a murder on Hammersmith Bridge in London in 1991.

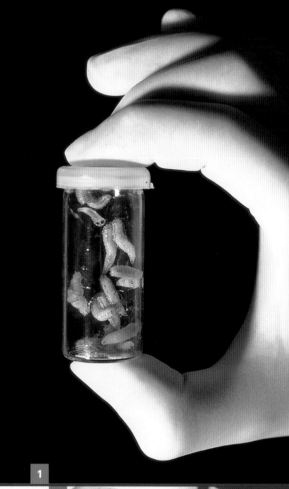

For example, the rate of growth of tree roots that have penetrated a skeleton will provide some relevant information.

Skeletons can themselves provide clues, since the rate at which nitrogen is lost from buried bones may be tested. However, results are likely to be imprecise because of variables such as temperature and water quantity in the soil.

IDENTIFYING THE VICTIM

Identification techniques may be critical in a homicide investigation with regard to both the victim and the suspect, and this is where forensic anthropology plays a crucial role. Identifying a skeleton lacking the skull first involves establishing that the bones are human rather than animal. Once this has been verified the age, sex, and height of the deceased needs to be determined. Skulls may be classified by their cephalic index, that is, the ratio of the maximum width to the maximum length. The more spherical the skull, the higher the index. The sutures on the skull provide clues to age, while differences between the skulls of men and women—for example in the nasal aperture, the shape of the eye sockets, and the slope of the forehead—all assist with identification. Skull identification was crucial to the arrest and conviction in 1935 of Dr. Buck Ruxton, who killed his wife and their maid, dismembered the bodies, and then left them in a ravine in Scotland. Forensic scientists developed a new technique during the course of their investigation: the negative from a photograph of Mrs. Ruxton was enlarged and an X-ray of the skull superimposed upon it—they matched exactly.

When the body of an unidentified victim is found, establishing gender is easier with an adult than an adolescent. In particular, the pelvic girdle differs substantially between grown men and grown women. The skeleton's age may, however, be easier to determine, at least approximately, in the case of a child because of the relative predictability of bone fusion or the arrival of adult teeth. It is often difficult to establish with ease the race or ethnic background, too, in part because of the incidence of interracial relations.

The human ear is conveniently distinctive and the pioneer criminologist Alphonse Bertillon long ago recognized its potential as a means of identification. So did Jacques Penry, inventor of the photo-fit. He made the point that an ear is as unique to a person as a fingerprint, while Alfred Ianarelli actually devised an eighteen-measurement system for identifying ears. Ear identification seldom features in crime fiction—perhaps its relevance is little known—but has sometimes cropped up in real cases. A notable example occurred in Berkeley, California, in 1925. Charles Henry Schwartz sought to fake his own death in an explosion at his chemical laboratory. But the dead man's ear was not a match for Schwartz's and the culprit was soon traced. He had killed an itinerant preacher and sought to remove means of identification such as fingertips, eyes, and teeth, leaving out, obviously, the all important ear.

Teeth may provide crucial evidence of identity, since they, and some materials used for fillings, are more durable than the rest of the human body. Furthermore, no two sets of teeth are the same. Teeth may also indicate the dead person's age, race, and (for instance in the case of expensive repair work) social status and wealth. The ready availability of dental records helps to facilitate this means of identification. Forensic odontology often plays a part in homicide investigation, a fact recognized in crime fiction as long ago as 1934: see Dorothy L. Sayers's story *In the Teeth of the Evidence*. Since no two sets of teeth are the same, a person's dental chart is as unique as his or her fingerprints and potentially as valuable for purposes of identification. Identification of criminals by bite marks has been accepted in court trials for about a century and marks left by Ted Bundy on the left buttock of one of his victims, Lisa Levy, played a significant role in the prosecution case against him. Remarkably difficult to destroy, teeth are often the only source of identification in cases of burned or severely mutilated corpses, as found after air crashes or bombings.

Cranio-facial reconstruction is a technique of steadily growing importance, thanks to the work of the Russian expert Mikhail Gerasimov and the British medical artist Richard Neave. Martin Cruz Smith made effective use of Gerasimov's work in his best-selling novel *Gorky Park* (1981). Neave's achievements in reconstructing the facial tissues of historical figures (such as Philip II, the father of Alexander the Great) from their skulls led to his becoming involved in homicide investigations. He makes use of known measurements of the thickness of soft tissue at key areas on human faces by creating a cast of the skull and inserting wooden pegs cut to lengths of the desired tissue thickness on the corresponding points of the skull. Finally, he plasters the cast with layers of clay matching the thickness specified by the pegs and makes final touches to simulate skin and tissue. Features such as the nose, lips, and eyelids are modeled on top, their shape being determined by the underlying muscles. Neave does not make excessive claims for his work; he regards his reconstructions as providing "a reasonable indication of how that person would have looked," but precision is impossible due to the number of potentially variable factors. Reconstructions may make use of sophisticated methods such as X-ray scanning and computer programs. The software can verify the reconstruction with available anthropological data, but details such as lips, ears, and noses still require conjecture.

PRESERVING EXHIBITS

An exhibit is an item of property that comes into the possession of the investigating team, whether or not it is eventually produced as evidence in court. Because the importance of the exhibit to the prosecution case may not be apparent at first, it is vital to take great care in keeping and identifying exhibits. This involves packing them properly and not only labeling each package but having them appropriately signed by witnesses who refer to it. The overriding aim must be to avoid contaminating exhibits—compromising DNA or other evidence found on them. Where items of clothing are taken from a body there may be a risk of contamination if the forensic scientist then takes further items from a different person. This can be addressed by having a different member of the team deal with each body from whom clothes are taken .

Audio, video, and closed-circuit tapes also need to be handled professionally. When a videotape is obtained it should be sealed, dated, and timed—without delay. The seal should also be signed by the person who has provided the tape. The officer responsible for dealing with exhibits must make sure that the tape is copied, the original re-sealed, and the labels noted accordingly. Tapes must be stored well away from strong electromagnetic fields that could damage them.

Items of property need to be preserved for examination by the appropriate forensic officers and documentary exhibits must be photocopied. Where the exhibits include cash, vehicles, or other valuable items, security is essential. Finally, exhibits must not be disposed of without the approval of an appropriate senior officer.

WEATHER CONDITIONS

Sometimes, forensic meteorologists can play a vital role in crime investigations. With the aid of computers they are able to "hindcast"—to establish whether claimed or apparent crime scenes match up to reality. For example, there may be an issue as to whether light levels were such as to enable a witness to see the offender well enough to provide a positive identification. Weather data may also help a forensic entomologist to offer an opinion about the time of death, such as in a case where a person must have been killed directly after he or she disappeared, but kept somewhere cooler in the meantime.

COMMUNICATIONS

The key to successful investigation lies in efficient communication: internally within the investigating team and its support network; and externally via the media. Common objectives include identifying the victim, appealing for witnesses, and locating suspects. If a case takes time to solve it may be important to keep it alive in the public mind with media assistance. These aims can be achieved in a variety of ways: with public appeals, and through careful management of the release of information to the general public.

If a murder victim's body cannot quickly be identified and an artist's impression or facial reconstruction has been prepared, an appeal— sensitively conducted through the media—can often prove helpful. Public appeals are most likely to be successful if they include specific detail: vague requests for help and cooperation are less likely to yield good results. When appealing for witnesses, therefore, it is important to be clear about the information that is being sought and to provide pointers that might help assist the memory of potential witnesses, such as details about times of day or particular locations. A better response may be achieved if the appeal is directed to specific groups of likely witnesses, perhaps people traveling to watch a sports event in the vicinity of the crime scene.

Similarly, requests to the public for details about a suspect who is sought are more likely to be successful if they deal with specifics and emphasize key reasons why people might wish to help, for instance in the case of a child murder, or if the killing was especially horrible.

Appeals via the media often have an important subtext: the murderer usually tries to keep tabs on the progress of investigations so it is worth sending an implicit message to the culprit that the police already possess significant evidence and are simply looking for the final pieces in the puzzle.

An artist's impression, a photograph, or security camera pictures featuring the offender can be of benefit. When a small boy, James Bulger, was abducted from a Liverpool shopping center in 1993 the security camera footage of his two young killers, leading him by the hand, made an enormous impact on the public consciousness and led to the early arrest of the culprits. In contrast, descriptions, drawings, e-fits, and so on, may acutally have a negative effect on the reliability of witnesses' recollections.

It is a good idea to provide detailed information about a suspect in cases where a photograph or video clip is unavailable since this reduces the chance of an innocent person mistakenly being treated as a suspect and exposing the police to claims for compensation.

Skilful use of the media helps to provide the public with appropriate reassurance or warnings where there is a dangerous killer on the loose and a serious risk of further crimes.

Typically, a major murder investigation will require regular, perhaps daily, media briefings. A decision needs to be made at the outset about who will brief the media. It is usually wise to withhold selected details of the killer's MO from the media; failure to do this may reduce the value of a later statement by a suspect containing information about the MO that would not generally have been known.

An audio or video record should be made of all media briefings, including any interviews on radio or television involving members of the investigating team. Copies of media releases need to be kept, together with a note of strategic decisions made in cooperation with the media, and the reasons for those decisions.

Sometimes the impact of an appeal via the media will be much greater if a person closely connected with the victim participates. There have been several cases in which an appeal has been made by the person who eventually proved to be the culprit. In 1994 Gordon Wardell claimed that he had been attacked, and his wife kidnaped and killed by robbers seeking to steal from the building society that she managed in a British town. He made an emotive appeal for information while still bearing the scars of the alleged assault. But it was later uncovered that he had a previous conviction for violence and that he was in fact the murderer of his wife, faking the supposed kidnaping and assault to throw investigators off his

trail. With such cases in mind, appeals of this kind may have an additional, unstated purpose: where a person close to the deceased (perhaps a husband or wife) is privately regarded by detectives as a prime suspect, asking that individual to participate in a public appeal may not only yield further information from witnesses but may also put the suspect under considerable personal pressure and, perhaps, expose weaknesses in the story that he or she has been telling.

Generally, treating the family of the victim with care and sensitivity is important not only for gathering important information, but also for welfare reasons and particularly in situations where community tensions are at work, such as in racially or sexually motivated cases. Even if an officer from the investigating police force is appointed as a contact with the family it may be a good idea to seek additional help from grief counsellors or other experts. Effective communications are vital at all times, but the desire to keep the family fully informed should not be allowed to compromise the integrity of the investigation.

RECONSTRUCTIONS

A physical reconstruction of the crime may help to open up new lines of investigation. A reconstruction can have a variety of aims, such as

1 The parents of missing eight-year-old Sarah Payne make a public appeal for information.
2 A still from the film *The Usual Suspects*, 1995.
3 Enhanced video of two youths wanted in connection with the murder of James Bulger, 1993.
4 Media representatives crowd round the West Yorkshire Chief Constable for news on the Yorkshire Ripper case in 1979.
5 Gordon Wardell, husband of murdered Carol Wardell, retraces the journey she made on the night she was abducted.
6 A reconstruction of the murder of Jayne McDonald, a victim of the Yorkshire Ripper.

jogging witnesses' memories, searching for fresh information or testing information that has already been provided to the investigation. Reconstructions often take place at the same time as the murder, and in the same place, but the following week, or, in a long-running investigation, on the anniversary of the murder. Increasingly, technology is being used to create virtual reconstructions and in several countries regular television programs are built around this technique in conjunction with public appeals for information.

A reconstruction presents logistical challenges: for example, enough dedicated telephone lines need to be set up to deal with calls if there is a good response from the public. The media considerations of a reconstruction need to be addressed by targeting the right audience and publicizing the proposed reconstruction. It is also important to deal sensitively with any concerns that the victim's family may have about retracing the steps of the crime.

EYEWITNESS EVIDENCE

Eyewitness evidence may seem compelling, but it is often flawed. The Oklahoma bombing in 1995 is a case in point. Timothy McVeigh and two accomplices, Terry Nichols and Michael Fortier, left a trail of forensic evidence—no one else did. Yet there has been much debate about John Doe 2, the supposed fourth man at the crime scene. The authorities' view is that John Doe 2 never existed outside the realm of conspiracy theory and it seems his alleged existence springs from witness speculation that there may have been an additional culprit.

Incorrect eyewitness testimony is the commonest cause of wrongful convictions: this view is borne out by convictions overturned on the basis of exclusionary DNA evidence that was originally obtained on the basis of eyewitness testimony. The problem is that the human memory is very malleable. This is illustrated by the bystander effect, where witnesses conclude that innocent bystanders committed the crimes. This comes as a result from the witness recalling having seen the bystander, but being unclear about the context.

The most reliable eyewitness evidence comes from observers who have had the chance to watch a suspect for a while, rather than catching a fleeting glimpse of a supposed culprit. Proper interviewing procedure is fundamental to recording accurate statements from the witnesses. The interviewer should avoid leading questions that suggest an answer. Interviews also need to be conducted promptly—before memories fade—and allow witnesses to freely recall what happened.

The weapon focus effect is one of the reasons for eyewitness inaccuracies. When you are staring at a gun or a knife, you may take little notice of the person wielding it. Another hazard is unconscious transference: we tend to see and hear what we expect to see and hear, but we often react positively to suggestions. So, in the case of an identification parade, there may be a tendency to assume that the culprit is in the lineup—even if that is not the case—and to make a selection from those who are present.

SEARCH

The conduct of searches is a feature of most murder investigations. As well as the scene where the crime was committed, there are many other places that need to be searched, such as the suspect's home, vehicle, and place of work. Where a crime has been committed outdoors, a strategic decision needs to be made regarding the area to be searched. It is usually preferable to search an area larger than appears to be absolutely necessary, since the possible waste of resources may be more than outweighed by the discovery of additional relevant evidence. Occasionally, members of the public or the military may become involved in a search. If members of the public are involved, there is a particular need for good organization and supervision. Involving the public may yield an unexpected dividend if (as sometimes happens) the offender volunteers to take part in the search.

Formulating a search strategy entails thinking about the objectives that the search is intended to achieve—for instance to find some or all of the following:

- forensic information
- the murder weapon
- property left by the victim or the offender
- evidence of the offender's escape route
- witnesses
- a body

Sometimes special equipment or resources are needed to facilitate a search. If a body is believed to be buried underground, digging equipment will be required. Dogs may also be used to locate a corpse, drugs, or other evidence.

It may be necessary to conduct a line search—or fingertip search—undertaken on hands and knees, to find small items of evidence where the use of a search dog is considered inappropriate. In wooded areas, metal detectors and radar may be required. Searches may be conducted underwater in sewers, cesspools, ponds, lakes, and rivers. Aerial searches are useful where a large area needs to be covered and thermal-imaging equipment can be utilized to identify the location of a body before

it has cooled down, or to indicate a place where the ground has been disturbed.

A search of premises may lead to the discovery of documents that require examination. The list of possibilities is endless, but it may include credit card receipts, bank statements, and pornography. Photographs, negatives, audio tapes, compact discs, cameras, and videos may also provide vital clues. Computers often contain information that an offender may mistakenly believe he has deleted. Expert technical help can be called upon to access deleted files that are still on a computer hard-drive. All evidence found during a search should be scrupulously handled, labeled, packaged, and logged. Finally, the conduct of searches sometimes raises issues about the health and safety of those conducting the search, so the strategy needs to include the adoption of proper safety standards.

SEARCH WARRANTS

Even authorized law enforcement officers will need, to have a search warrant in order to search premises without consent. Warrants are issued by a judge—the precise rules vary depending on the location—and the judge needs to be satisfied that there is probable cause, in other words that there is reason to believe that items relevant to the investigation will be found in the location to be searched. Detectives generally require warrants to be drafted in broad terms: if, for example, a warrant extends to a garage but not to any vehicle parked inside it, a car or van found in the garage cannot be searched under the warrant.

HOUSE-TO-HOUSE CANVASSES

House-to-house canvasses often provide investigators with important information. The problem is that they can be costly and, if poorly focused, unsuccessful. Good management of house-to-house canvasses involves clearly defining where the canvass is to be made, taking crucial data—significant sightings and discoveries of evidence—into account in choosing the area for the inquiries. The next step is to case the area to establish details of the properties within it.

The information to be gleaned from house-to-house canvasses is variable. It may range from collecting general intelligence to identifying the prime suspect. Investigators should be fully debriefed and the team ready to respond fast if the canvass produces significant fresh information that might lead to an arrest.

IDENTIFICATION STRATEGY

A key part of a murder investigation is the identification of the offender. Sometimes identification is disputed and evidence challenged in court. Many jurisdictions have detailed practical rules about matters of identification and investigators need to be aware of those rules.

Where identification is disputed, some or all of the following points may be relevant:

- for how long did the witness observe the accused?
- what was the distance between them?
- how good was the light?
- had the witness ever seen the accused before?
- how much time elapsed between the original observation and the subsequent identification?
- was there any significant discrepancy between the description of the accused given when the witness was first questioned and the actual appearance of the accused?

When a suspect's description becomes available, it should be noted and used as part of the identification process. Failure to do so may open up identification evidence to challenge.

Reliable identification requires more than simple recognition. Where the identity of the offender is unknown one possibility is to take a witness to a particular neighborhood to see whether the offender can be identified there. Alternatively, the witness may be shown photographs or videotape in the hope of securing an identification.

Facial imaging may play a part. This involves creating an image of the offender and can be produced in various ways:

- an artist's impression produced where there is no witness available to be interviewed
- an artist composite put together following a cognitive interview where the witness is asked to recall the appearance of the offender
- computerized imaging, again based on a description provided in a cognitive interview
- illustrated facial imaging based on photographic elements chosen by the witness from a catalog
- facial mapping, a relatively new technique using the comparison of poor quality photographs with photographs of known suspects

1 A selection of photo-fit images compiled in an attempt to identify the Yorkshire Ripper.
2 Police undertake a fingertip search of the area surrounding one of the Yorkshire Ripper's victims.
3 A specialist criminal portrait artist makes a composite image of a suspect.
4 A technician studies genetic fingerprints on a computer monitor.

It is important not to disclose facial images outside of the team to avoid any suggestion that witnesses have been influenced in their recollections. If differing facial images are produced by a number of witnesses, publication of these images can be misleading; the best bet is to publicize the image considered to be the most accurate.

Where the police have enough information to justify arresting a particular suspect, identification evidence may be derived from lineup, group identification, video identification, or (but only as a last resort) by confronting the witness with the suspect. Lineups can be problematical, for instance, where it proves difficult to find enough people with a resemblance to the suspect. Difficulties of this kind raise questions about whether makeup can be used to effect minor changes to the appearance of the people in the lineup. It is important not to go too far, for example by changing the ethnic appearance of a participant.

Voice identification can provide limited assistance in some cases by supplying corroborative evidence of identification. Voice identification should be carried out as soon as possible after the commission of the crime. If a suspect agrees, it is helpful to come as close as possible to the exact words spoken at the time of the crime. Volunteers who have a similar dialect to the suspect's may be invited to a recording session. It is helpful to have the help of a linguistics expert, and it is best to make voice samples in a similar context—in conversation as opposed to reading a scripted statement.

DNA profiling has, in a short time, become the most powerful tool in the forensic detective's kit. Yet if it is true that in a civilized society it is better for ninety-nine guilty men to be acquitted than one innocent man convicted, perhaps DNA profiling is at least as important for its ability to prove innocence as culpability. Many prisoners—some of them on Death Row—have been released following DNA evidence that they should not have been convicted in the first place.

DEALING WITH SUSPECTS

In some cases investigators may wish to identify a group of potential suspects by virtue of the MO employed in the murder, and previous recorded crimes with similar features. The risk is that the potential group of suspects may be too large to be dealt with efficiently. Careful assessment of the crime scene, as well as the MO of suspects, is therefore vital. Suspects may be chosen from those who:

> **live or work within a defined radius of the crime scene**
> **are known or believed to frequent the area of the crime scene**
> **had access to the victim**

An important question concerns the circumstances in which a suspect should be eliminated from the investigation. There have been too many cases over the years where an eliminated suspect has ultimately been proved to be the culprit. The reasons for considering elimination of the suspect may need to be

1 A surveillance squad in the Metro in Paris.
2 FBI agent Mark Wilson loads DNA samples in a DNA sequencer.

weighed up: for example, an alibi given by a husband or wife may be much less compelling as a reason for elimination than DNA evidence that excludes the suspect.

Any alibi should be investigated promptly, thoroughly and without any bias. There should be no ambiguity in an alibi; it is widely regarded as good procedure to have the suspect agree to record the details of the alibi on a tape.

SURVEILLANCE

Homicide investigations often entail surveillance of witnesses or suspects. Surveillance methods have become increasingly sophisticated in recent years as a result of advances in technology. Surveillance typically involves monitoring both the movements and behavior of one or more people. The most common types are visual and audio surveillance, but this means much more than merely watching or eavesdropping in a conventional way. Surveillance may be either overt or covert, that is, with or without the subject's knowledge.

Visual surveillance may involve observing the target through cameras, video cameras, or closed-circuit television. Audio surveillance (or bugging), may involve the use of a listening device to overhear or record a private conversation. Frequently, a device such as a VCR enables both audio and visual surveillance to be undertaken. Tracking devices installed in vehicles, on people, or on objects emit signals that can be monitored by the investigators. This is less labor intensive than traditional visual surveillance and allows for precise monitoring from a considerable distance. The prevalence of personal computers has led to a marked increase in computer surveillance, for example by monitoring e-mail communications.

Although surveillance is invaluable in many investigations, not least because recordings made through surveillance can be produced as evidence at a trial, civil rights groups have long expressed concerns about the adverse social effects of invading people's privacy. Many jurisdictions have developed increasingly elaborate legal rules governing the use of surveillance, including the interception of communications by computer. Legal rules about personal privacy are often subject to exceptions in the field of crime detection, but investigators need to take care not to violate applicable laws, since this could damage the prospects of winning a conviction.

INTERVIEWING STRATEGY

The interviewing of witnesses and suspects must not be haphazard. An interview should be structured with care in the light of relevant evidence already collected. Each interview must be conducted fairly, so as to minimize the risk that the interviewing process will be contested at a later trial.

The purpose of the interview should always be kept in mind: it is to obtain accurate and reliable information from the interviewee. Information given by an interviewee should be compared with what is already known or what can be established. The interview should be conducted ethically and without preconceived ideas. This does not, however, mean that legitimate persistence in questioning is unacceptable. Even if an interviewee chooses to remain silent, it may be proper to keep pressing relevant questions. Children or other vulnerable interviewees must be treated with particular care and consideration.

It is not only legitimate, but in many cases positively desirable, for the interviewing officer to make use of an aide memoire—a memory jogger—to provide reference points for the questioning. Advice from an expert psychological profiler may also help to determine how the interview is handled.

INTERVIEWING PRINCIPLES

Interviewing often begins at the crime scene itself. Law enforcement officers are accustomed to questioning people who fall into four broad categories: complainants, victims, witnesses, and suspects. In homicide investigations the focus is usually narrowed into witnesses and suspects.

Proper preparation is the secret of success in interviewing. However, there is often little time to prepare in advance for interviews at the crime scene. Investigators will have to rely on their training and the strength of their interviewing techniques in such situations. At the crime scene, the investigating officer may be the first person to whom the witness speaks. It is important, therefore, for the interviewer to be aware of the trauma that the witness may have suffered as a result of being present in the vicinity of a homicide and the witness should be made comfortable, but at the same time handled professionally. If possible, it is a good idea to have the witness seated in a neutral environment, away from the ongoing investigative activity.

Good interviewers seek to develop a rapport with witnesses. A positive, friendly, and respectful approach, showing genuine interest in and awareness of the witness's concerns, will pay off, especially if the witness is nervous or frightened during the interview. Witnesses should always be interviewed separately and without delay.

The effective interviewer will:

- be a good listener, using appropriate body language to show interest and to create rapport
- be adaptable, taking account of the witness's cultural or ethnic background and experiences
- be sympathetic yet detached
- be patient and avoid pressuring the witness into saying something that is incorrect or misleading
- show confidence (but not arrogance)
- avoid preconceived ideas and prejudices
- have all the available information about the crime
- phrase questions so as to obtain information related to the relevant aspect of the crime
- speak clearly and without rushing
- keep questions simple

COGNITIVE INTERVIEWING

The constant search for ways to improve the quality of information gathered from interviewing has led law enforcement officers worldwide to study and practice cognitive interviewing techniques. At its simplest, cognitive interviewing is a way of jogging the witness's memory with a view to gaining more vivid and reliable details from them. The aim is to ask questions that elicit a descriptive response. Put another way, the essence of cognitive interviewing is that it is as important to ask the witness questions in a particular way as it is to select the best questions in the first place.

The theory and practice of cognitive interviewing is continuing to develop, and a variety of approaches can be adopted. One view is that it is important for the meeting to take place in the witness's own home, since this is most likely to put the person at ease.

Where the main purpose of the interview is to obtain a description of the suspect, the interviewer may start by explaining the difference between recognizing someone and remembering someone. Recognition is based on seeing an image or likeness, hearing the person's voice, or seeing him or her again. Remembering is more difficult: the development of a picture in the mind without external stimulus. Remembering is potentially more valuable.

A favorite method, once a rapport has begun to be established, is to take the witness back to a time some hours before the crime was committed. Rather than speaking about the murder itself at this stage, the aim is to encourage the witness to remember what led up to it, reconstructing the circumstances by recalling as many details as possible. At this stage of the interview the emphasis may be on the witness's environment at the time, and his or her feelings or reactions to events of the day. Interviewers ask witnesses not to leave anything out of the story, even if particular details seem trivial. A minor incident that appears to be irrelevant may help the witness to remember something else about a vital facet of the case. So the golden rule that interviewers need to teach witnesses is to report everything.

There are various practical ways of remembering physical appearance. In trying to recall what someone looks like, it often helps to ask whether the person reminds the witness of another person—and why. There may be something unusual about the person, for example a tattoo or injury, which has stuck in the memory. It is also a good idea to review the person from top to bottom, with reference to such matters as:

hair (including the amount as opposed to merely the length)
shape and color of the eyes
amount and position of the eyebrows
shape of the nose
shape of the lips
shape of the whole face
tone and shade of the skin

Other crucial features may include:

accent
voice
physical mannerisms
condition of hands

Cognitive interviewing is sometimes conducted by an officer who is trained as a composite image artist. The officer seeks to gather as much detail from the witness as possible before beginning to create an image, either by hand sketching or by using a catalog of pre-drawn physical characteristics. The witness judges the image produced for accuracy and changes are made to ensure that it is as close as possible to the witness's recollection. Once satisfied, the witness signs and dates the likeness so that it can be passed to the investigative team for further action.

Although cognitive interviewing has gained rapidly in popularity with law enforcement officers recently, like any other technique of detection, it has limitations. It is often difficult to apply the textbook principles when conducting a real-life interview. Also the technique is time consuming and homicide investigation teams often find that time is in very short supply. If too much time is spent interviewing each witness, there is a risk that other potentially valuable witnesses will not be seen soon enough after the crime.

HYPNOSIS

There are parallels between cognitive interviewing and the more controversial technique of investigative hypnosis. An added problem is that, in many countries, evidence obtained from a witness under hypnosis may be subject to legal challenge at a subsequent murder trial and may not be admissible at all as evidence. In any case, where hypnosis is contemplated—for example, where the witness suffered a particularly serious trauma as a result of seeing murder committed—stringent safeguards need to be taken, both to ensure the well-being of the witness and the fairness of the information obtained through this method. Hypnosis should therefore be conducted by a qualified and highly skilled practitioner and additional precautions, such as videotaping the procedure, need to be considered.

INTERVIEWING IN PRACTICE

Interviewing a suspect in a homicide case requires tact, skill, and professionalism. Incompetent interviewing may fail to secure evidence adequate to justify prosecution, or may jeopardize a subsequent trial if it appears that the suspect's civil rights were violated. It follows that any officer interviewing a suspect should have a thorough understanding of the rules of evidence and the legal rights of a murder suspect. It is equally important for the interviewing officer to have detailed knowledge of the crime, including the contents of the crime scene, the statements of key witnesses, and the details of principal exhibits (clothing, weapons etc.).

The investigating team may prepare a personal history folder on the suspect that is separate from the evidence file; recording the suspect's personal and family details, and any known indiosyncracies. In a homicide case, where more resources will be devoted to the investigation than with other crimes, a single officer may be in charge of researching and preparing the personal history folder. Small details can be telling, even if not directly relevant to the crime, since, if carefully used in the interview, they may help to convince the suspect that the interviewer already knows a great deal about him or her and is able to find out even more.

Typically, a suspect will be interviewed by two officers and they need to reach agreement on the interview plan beforehand. Where possible, it helps to prepare the interview room: extraneous noise is a distraction to be avoided; the suspect should not be able to hear conversations taking place outside the room; the suspect should be seated with his or her back to the door of the room, so that if anyone comes in and makes a signal to the interviewers, the suspect cannot observe it; the room should not contain either a clock or a telephone, since these may cause distractions. The interviews are usually taped in accordance with local laws and practice and an audio-visual link to another room enables other members of the investigating team to observe proceedings, perhaps including superior officers who may be able to advise on technique and strategy when needed.

1 Sergeant Thomas Winn of the Camillus PD uses new software to make a composite drawing of people for police work.
2 A sheriff's deputy books a suspect in Clinton County, Maryland.
3 A woman in a hypnotic trance, characterized by susceptibility to suggestion.
4 Sharon Stone in the film *Basic Instinct*, being interviewed by murder investigators.
5 Elizabeth Short with Major Matt Gordon in 1947. About fifty men claimed to have killed her and the case remains unsolved.

Broadly speaking, there are two types of technique for interrogating a suspect, depending on whether or not the interviewer is confident of the suspect's guilt. This division is reflected in the two main facets of the interview. The first is the inquisitorial stage, where the interviewer is seeking information, both verbal and non-verbal, which will lead to the truth. The second stage is that of persuasion, where an attempt is made to overcome the suspect's resistance to questioning.

For the interviewer, a crucial question is whether the suspect is trying to decide whether to admit or deny the crime. Law enforcement officers are trained to seek confessions from culprits; but false confessions, even to serious crimes such as homicide, are surprisingly common. The still unsolved Black Dahlia case, the killing of Elizabeth Short in Los Angeles in 1947 has attracted about fifty confessions, including some from people who were not even born at the time of the murder. A confession obtained through illegal means, such as physical threats, will usually not be admitted by the court. So quiet, subtle persuasion is called for.

There are various effective techniques of persuasion that can be usefully employed:

> **persuaders tend to be most effective if they are perceived as having high status and therefore a good appearance, an efficient approach, and even good manners are worth cultivating**
>
> **the interviewer must retain credibility in the eyes of the suspect at all times**
>
> **persuasion is more effective if the suspect actively participates in the interrogation (although a risk is that if a suspect is allowed to lie persistently, it could become harder to persuade him later to change his mind and tell the truth)**
>
> **a suspect's behavior may be better influenced by the interviewer if, at the start of the interview, statements are put forward with which the suspect is known to agree**
>
> **persuasion may be more effective if the suspect is uncertain or apprehensive due to lack of information (but subjecting the suspect to excessive pressure may be counter-productive, both in practice and in terms of compromising the legality of the interrogation)**

A crucial skill for the interviewing officer is the ability to determine when the suspect is lying. In many jurisdictions it is legitimate, in certain circumstances, to make use of a lie detector, also known as a polygraph. But there are other ways in which experienced detectives may seek to determine whether a suspect is telling lies. Physical symptoms such as sweating, lip-licking, yawning, facial tics, nervous coughing, and changes in the pupils of the eye may all be suggestive of an attempt to conceal the truth (and such physical symptoms are, in effect, also measured scientifically when a polygraph is used).

Displacement activity may also provide a clue to dishonesty. It takes varying forms, such as:

> fidgeting
> fiddling with hands or fingers
> foot tapping
> biting fingernails or lip
> excessive smoking

Apart from physical signs, a liar may seek to compensate for dishonesty by giving excessive assurances of truthfulness—"I swear on my baby's life." An alternative approach is the defiant challenge where the suspect says, in effect, "prove it."

A subtler response is when the suspect merely says he or she can't remember. Alternative non-confrontational ways of avoiding the truth are to try to prey on the sympathy of the interviewer or simply to offer a bland and meaningless response.

The most sensitive and important phase of interrogation usually comes when the suspect starts to consider whether it would be in his or her own interests to admit guilt. There are various signals that suggest to the experienced interrogator that the suspect has reached this point, for example:

> **requesting information**
> **attempting to bargain**
> **signs of arousal (such as tears or anger)**
> **partial agreement**
> **body language**
> **delay in replying**

If the officer conducting the interview sees that the suspect is considering confessing, the next step is to encourage that confession. Again, it is essential to comply with applicable legal rules, for example by avoiding threats or unlawful inducements. A simple method is to seek to minimize the advantages of denying guilt, perhaps by suggesting that denial may make matters worse for the suspect. It is helpful, so far as it is permissible to do so, to point out the advantages of confession and to indicate that the downside of confession is perhaps not as great as the suspect may think.

PSYCHIC DETECTION

High profile murder cases always attract cranks. The question that often arises is whether people who contact the police to put their psychic powers at the disposal of the investigating team should be treated seriously or not. At the height of the Yorkshire Ripper investigation many psychics responded to appeals in the tabloid press with telepathically-derived leads. The police appointed a psychic liaison to sift through the material that came in, but the case was ultimately solved in a conventional manner. An American medium, Nancy Myers, reportedly claims to have solved two hundred crimes. But the most noted psychic detective was Peter Hurkos, who achieved world wide prominence as a result of his brief involvement in the Boston Strangler case. He is said to have developed his powers after fracturing his skull in an accident. His skill lay in forming mental pictures of past or future events associated with people, places, or objects and he developed it to a point where the police sought his assistance. He contributed to the detection of a double killing in Miami and by the 1960s he was supposed to have had a role in twenty-seven solved murder cases across seventeen countries. His help was enlisted in the hunt for the Boston Strangler, but led detectives to someone who, although on the list of suspects, had no connection with the crimes. After a week on the case Hurkos departed, and three days later he was arrested on a charge of impersonating an FBI agent. This episode does not mean that psychic detection is necessarily useless in all circumstances, but the overwhelming majority of detectives rightly focus on more conventional methods of detection.

BRAIN FINGERPRINTING

The new technique of brain fingerprinting, pioneered by Dr. Larry Farwell and tested at the FBI Academy at Quantico, may provide investigators with more assistance than psychic detection. Brain fingerprinting is based on a simple principle: memory centers in the brain respond to direct stimuli. The response is called a murmur— when a subject sees something, activity occurs in the brain. When the subject recognizes what is seen, there is a murmur. The response of the brain can be measured by electrodes attached to the subject's head that are linked to brain fingerprinting software. The key to success is to ask the right questions. Investigators need to phrase those questions so that when a murmur occurs, the reason is clear. For example, both a killer and an innocent person might respond to the sight of a murder weapon. What is needed is a response that reflects guilty knowledge. There is an obvious parallel with the polygraph, which measures physical responses, but brain fingerprinting takes the process a step further by revealing responses that the subject cannot control. However, like any other detection technique, brain fingerprinting plainly has limitations: it can reveal the presence of electrical activity in the brain, but not detailed information about what is stored there. How brain fingerprinting will work with a person suffering from psychosis or a head injury is as yet unclear. Evidence derived from brain fingerprinting is currently inadmissible in murder cases in the U.S., but the idea's potential is great. In a murder case where there are no witnesses and only the culprit has detailed knowledge of the crime, for instance, it may even be that the brain will one day become a witness for the prosecution.

ARREST

An arrest involves depriving someone of his or her freedom and a mistake in the arrest procedure can jeopardize the whole case. Moreover, a wrongful arrest can lead to potentially costly litigation, as well as damage public confidence in law enforcement.

All this means that it is vital to be able to demonstrate compelling reasons to justify an arrest. The legal implications, which vary from state to state, have to be addressed, and it is important to document the reasons for the arrest. Possible reasons are innumerable but may include:

- the fact that the suspect is known to have been at the crime scene when the crime was committed
- the suspect's history of using an MO similar to that adopted in the crime
- implicating evidence
- descriptions from witnesses corresponding to the suspect

Sometimes an arrest may be made immediately. When this is not the case it is generally good to research the suspect, with a view to establishing:

- a physical description of the suspect
- whether the suspect has a history of violence
- whether the suspect has access to weapons
- whether the suspect has access to other premises
- the suspect's lifestyle and associates
- the vehicles to which the suspect has access
- the suspect's criminal record
- a plan of the premises in which the arrest is likely to take place
- details of telephones within those premises
- the likely impact of the arrest on the immediate local community

Peter Hurkos who used psychic detection to help investigators track down the Boston Strangler.

Information generated by research may highlight potential safety risks to the arresting officers and may raise questions as to the extent to which they should be armed

Proper planning of an arrest covers administrative issues such as making sure that the premises where the arrest has taken place are appropriately guarded, and the obtaining of any special equipment necessary to force entry to the premises, if access is not given voluntarily. It may be sensible to have the arrest videotaped.

The law enforcement officers who participate in the arrest need to be properly briefed so that they are aware of the circumstances of the crime and have a thorough and up-to-date description of the suspect. They should know why the arrest is being made, as well as when, and where the suspect is to be taken once arrested.

If, following arrest, the suspect appears to have injuries, photographs should be taken of them. The suspect's clothing and footwear should be removed and the suspect thoroughly examined by a suitably trained and qualified physician. The suspect's fingerprints should be taken, together with front and profile photographs.

Following the arrest, the officers involved should be debriefed, especially regarding any information that has been given to them by the suspect. Significant debriefing data needs to be passed on quickly to those involved in any search of the premises where the arrest took place or in the interviewing of the suspect.

PROTECTING WITNESSES

The work of detectives does not finish once a person has been charged with murder. There needs to be continuing close liaison with the prosecutors and regular case conferences. It is also important to make sure that the prosecution case is not damaged, for example if key witnesses decide not to give evidence.

Witnesses may suffer intimidation, typically from associates of the accused who want to discourage them from testifying. Witness protection may therefore be required. This can involve a variety of measures, including the provision of a panic alarm or even relocation to a safe house. This is a costly precaution but may be essential to protect all the hard work devoted to solving the case.

1 A colored magnetic resonance image (MRI) scan through a human head, showing the brain in coronal section.
2 Police take down a teenager who led them on a dangerous car chase through the streets of Fort Lauderdale in Miami.
3 O.J. Simpson photographed by police after his arrest in connection with the murder of his wife.

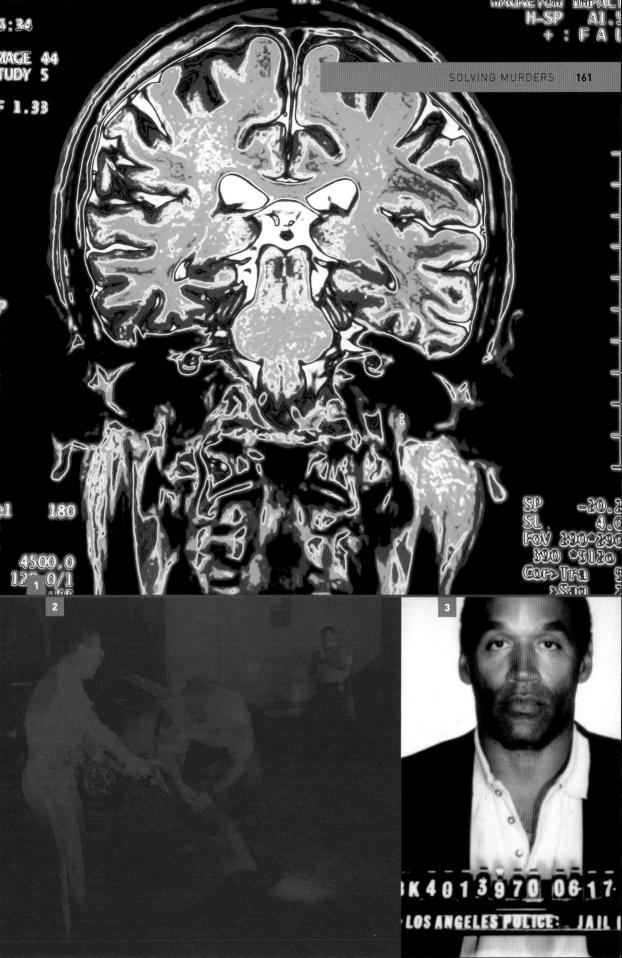

THE UNABOMBER

A series of bombings that began in 1978 led to a massive hunt for a culprit whom the FBI code-named the Unabomber (because his early targets were universities and airlines). The Unabomber proved remarkably elusive, with no apparent motive for his crimes: he made no ransom demands and he acted sporadically, showing himself as a man prepared to wait and plan between attacks.

The psychological profiler John Douglas joined the investigation after the fourth incident, when the president of an airline had been injured after opening a package addressed to him at home. The case was complicated: the first bomb had been directed at an eminent academic with no known enemies, the second had no obvious individual target, and the third had been intended to destroy a Boeing 727 in mid-flight. The key elements of the preliminary profile were that he was an obsessive-compulsive white man with above-average intelligence and significant technical ability.

Further bombings occurred again at irregular intervals: at one point the Unabomber was quiet for almost three years before an explosion in Berkeley in May 1985 disabled a student. Later that year the owner of a computer store in Sacramento was killed by a nail bomb that had been personally delivered. After another long gap a package bomb seriously injured a Californian professor in June 1993. A similar crime followed in Connecticut two days later. By now the bombs were being constructed with a high level of sophistication.

The general manager of an advertising agency in New Jersey was killed by another bomb in December 1994. The following April, the *New York Times* received a letter explaining that the agency had been targeted for "manipulating people's attitudes" and in further letters the

Unabomber expressed his anger about the ways in which technology was changing the world. The letters suggested that the author was part of a political group, but this was obviously a ploy: the crimes had the marks of a disaffected loner. As the correspondence continued, the Unabomber demanded that major newspapers publish a lengthy manifesto of his beliefs. These letters provided profilers with crucial information: the Unabomber was emerging, in Douglas's words, as a "messed-up ... failed academic" who needed to depersonalize others to justify his crimes. The FBI decided that it would be helpful to publish the manifesto—this was a controversial decision since it provoked the criticism that the culprit was being turned into a media celebrity and being rewarded for his crimes. But using the media proved successful: a social worker named David Kaczynski recognized phrases used by his eccentric brother Theodore, a former academic who lived like a hermit in a cabin in Montana. The cabin was raided and evidence of Theodore's guilt found. The profile proved correct: the bomber had become a professor of mathematics at Berkeley but, unable to cope, dropped out and became increasingly reclusive and embittered, an inadequate eccentric whose plan was to maim and kill so as to make other people as unhappy as he was.

Handcuffed and with his feet chained, the Unabomber is led into court.

MURDEROUS EYES

On the evening of December 1, 1996, officers from West Mercia Police found a woman kneeling in a country lane near a parked car. She was cradling the head of a man. Both of them were covered in blood, but the man was dead. She said that her name was Tracie Andrews and that the dead man was her boyfriend, Lee Harvey. They had gone out for a drink and on the way home had passed a black Ford Sierra car, which proceeded to chase them. The cars eventually stopped and Lee got out to confront the other driver. At that point a passenger in the Sierra, a fat man with "staring eyes" had jumped out and started stabbing Lee. Tracie tried to intervene and suffered a cut eyebrow and bruises as a result. The black car had then been driven off.

News of the "road rage" murder shocked the British public. Within two days, still bruised and distraught, Tracie Andrews made a televised appeal for the Sierra driver to come forward. "You are not to blame," she sobbed, "because you walked away." But no witnesses said that they had seen the Sierra. On the contrary, two men who had seen Harvey and Andrews driving along when the chase was supposed to be occurring had seen no other vehicle, let alone a Sierra in hot pursuit. Andrews took an overdose of pills and said it was because she could not bear to live without her lover, but other witnesses emerged who said that the couple's relationship had been stormy and that Andrews had hit Lee Harvey over the head with a bottle and punched him for visiting a nightclub without her. A previous boyfriend claimed that she had threatened him with a knife.

Investigators then turned to forensic data, which was to prove important. The pattern of blood on Andrews's clothing and the location of blood at the scene did not jibe with her account. A clump of her hair, pulled out at the roots, was found on the body and others had been stuck between Harvey's thumb and forefinger, suggesting a struggle. A bloodstained mark, matching Harvey's DNA profile, was found inside one of Andrews's ankle boots. The mark was about the size of a knife, parts of which were found near the corpse. This discovery helped police deduce why no weapon was present at the scene: they believed that she had stuffed it down her boot and threw it in a hospital wastebasket later. Furthermore a child who heard an argument near the murder scene claimed to hear only two voices, one of which was soft, like a woman's.

The police thought that Andrews had killed her lover in a violent fit. The fact that Harvey had nearly forty separate wounds showed that this was no quick quarrel after a driving incident. Andrews's defense maintained the "road rage" claim. The jury found her guilty and she was sentenced to life imprisonment. An appeal based on prejudicial pretrial publicity failed.

1 Tracie Andrews illustrates the staring eyes of her supposed murdered boyfriend's assailant in a news conference.
2 The blood-stained boot of Tracie Andrews showing where she kept the knife having stabbed her boyfriend to death.

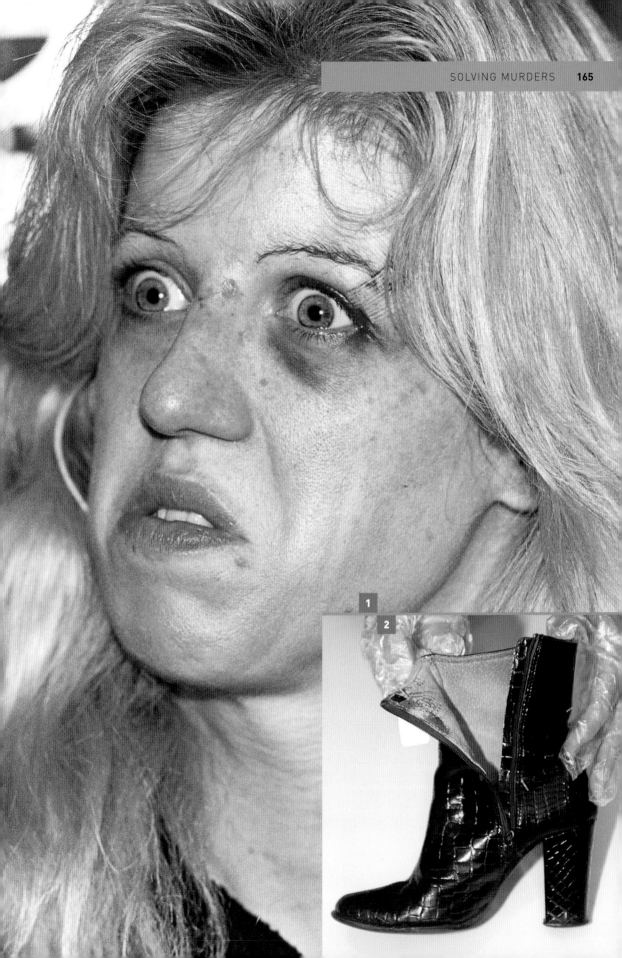

JUSTICE BITES BACK

Theodore "Ted" Bundy was an intelligent, good-looking, and charming man whose career as a serial killer was remarkable if only because of the risks that he took. His case shows that, even where investigators correctly identify a murderer, bringing the case to a successful conclusion can be long and difficult.

Between January and July 1974, Bundy was a student in Seattle. Young girls were repeatedly assaulted during that time and eight vanished altogether. Witnesses saw him accosting girls by the lake and he was overheard introducing himself as "Ted" to Janice Ott, whose remains were later found two miles away. From the many descriptions that were given, police were able to develop a photofit likeness of the prime suspect and the Seattle newspapers carried pictures of him. The police received many calls suggesting that the man resembled Bundy. But the list of suspects was long and it was thought unlikely that a man who approached girls with a view to abducting them would use his own name in the hearing of others. This was perhaps a logical view, but it was mistaken.

When Bundy moved to Utah, the disappearances in Seattle stopped, but a wave of killings in Salt Lake City began. He was arrested in August 1975 when police stopped his car and found in it a steel bar, a pair of handcuffs, a knit balaclava, and a mask made from pantyhose. Carol DaRonch, whom he had kidnaped but who managed to escape, picked Bundy's photograph from a set of mug shots. Along with two other witnesses, she watch a police lineup: despite the fact that Bundy had shaved off his moustache, had his hair cut short, and changed his hair parting, all three witnesses identified him. He was found guilty of abducting Carol, but escaped before his trial for murder could take place. Swiftly recaptured, he escaped again and embarked on a spree of robberies and murders in Florida. Not until February 1978 was he re-arrested, when a patrolman saw a car being driven erratically one morning: it was a stolen vehicle and when the driver was ordered to get out, he attacked the patrolman before being overpowered.

At his trial, Bundy pleaded not guilty, but an impression of his teeth fitted a bite mark on one of his victims and a mask he had dropped in the room of a girl he had attacked was identical to one found in the stolen car. He was sentenced to death in the electric chair, but remained on Death Row for a decade before his eventual execution in 1989. He may have killed as many as forty women. While in prison, Bundy experts offered his views on the nature of serial killers. In his opinion, overconfidence often leads to their capture, rather than (as is commonly supposed) a secret desire to be caught. According to Bundy, the usual motive for serial killing is the sheer thrill that the culprits derive from committing their crimes.

1 Ted Bundy looks pensive in court, awaiting the verdict of the jury.
2 The mass murderer finds something funny during a conversation with chief public defender Mike Minerva, right.

1

2

A GUILTY HAND

In July 1991, an eighteen-year-old Yorkshire girl, Julie Dart, who occasionally worked as a prostitute, disappeared. The police received a ransom note saying that if £145,000 (two hundred thousand U.S. dollars) was not paid, Julie would die. Shortly afterwards her naked body was found in a field: she had been hit on the head and strangled. Further letters from the same correspondent who described Julie's abduction as a "game," were sent to the police, demanding money and threatening further abductions of prostitutes. British Rail received a blackmail note, apparently from the same source, saying that a high-speed express would be derailed unless £200,000 (two hundred and eighty thousand U.S. dollars) was paid.

On January 22, 1992, a young real estate agent named Stephanie Slater was kidnaped while showing a property in Birmingham to a client who had given the name of Southwall. Her employers received a ransom demand for £175,000 (two-hundred and fifty thousand U.S. dollars) and tape-recorded messages made by Stephanie at the insistence of her captor. Working closely with the police, a colleague of Stephanie's took the ransom money along the convoluted route devised by the kidnaper, but he lost contact with the detectives. Although one thousand men from six police forces and vast resources had been deployed in an attempt to capture the kidnaper, his ingenious plan worked and he escaped with the money. Stephanie was released and attention focused on the hunt for the criminal. The police were confident that the kidnaper was the same man who had killed Julie Dart.

Despite his cleverness and the elaborate precautions he took to disguise his identity, the kidnaper had provided his hunters with important clues. The letters were written in a distinctive style, complete with misspellings and unusual grammar. Even more importantly, his voice had been tape-recorded when he gave instructions to the real-estate agents. Finally, witnesses had seen

him, and police artists produced two sketches based on their observations. A much-publicized appeal for information was made on BBC Television's *Crimewatch U.K.* program. The tape was played and the sketches shown. A woman telephoned to say that she believed the voice was that of her former husband, Michael Sams. Her story was convincing but she said that Sams had an artificial leg that caused him to limp—and none of the witnesses had mentioned this. When detectives visited Sams at his workshop in Nottinghamshire—where Stephanie had been held captive—they saw a man with a startling resemblance to the faces in the sketches. Sams confessed to Stephanie's kidnaping, but he claimed that Julie Dart had been murdered by an accomplice whom he refused to name. The letters written in the Dart case were similar to those in the Slater case: he admitted writing the Dart letters, but said he had done so at his friend's insistence. He was found guilty of both crimes and promptly admitted that he had killed Julie Dart.

1 An artist's impression, issued by police, of the man they believe kidnaped Stephanie Slater and killed Julie Dart in 1992.
2 Michael Sams under arrest.

BURIED EVIDENCE

In August 1991, a builder named Frederick West was charged with sexual offences against several of his children. The case did not proceed because his daughter decided not to give evidence for the prosecution. A woman police officer became concerned when the daughter said that she was afraid she would finish up "in the back garden" like her sister Heather. Heather had been missing for four years. The police obtained a search warrant for the premises owned by West and his wife Rosemary, at 25 Cromwell Road, Gloucester. They decided to dig up the back garden and arrested the Wests.

West confessed to murdering Heather and described precisely where he had buried her. An elaborate excavation took place and ground-penetrating radar was used to scan for disturbances in the earth. Heather's skull was discovered and further human remains were soon found, including a decomposed fetus and several dismembered bodies. Several teenage girls who had disappeared over many years were, thanks to expert pathological work, identified as victims. Infrared spectroscopy helped to determine the length of time that the corpses had been buried underground. It developed that West's first wife, her daughter, and a friend also could not be accounted for; the bodies of the daughter and friend were subsequently found in fields a few miles away. West was charged with twelve murders and Rosemary with ten. West contended that he alone was guilty (although he said in one interview that his wife had buried bodies in the cellar of the house). He committed suicide by hanging himself in prison on New Year's Day, 1995.

The prosecution accepted that the evidence against Rosemary West was circumstantial—this has been described as the "she must have known" case. The prosecution claimed that the husband and wife had a mutual obsession with sex, including violent sex. As long ago as 1973 the

couple had been arrested after beating and sexually abusing a sixteen-year-old girl, but the victim had been too frightened to give evidence. The Wests were therefore only convicted of indecent assault and actual bodily harm and the magistrate fined them each a paltry twenty-five pounds (about forty U.S. dollars). It may have been the experience of the case that prompted the Wests to kill their subsequent victims, for fear of being reported again to the police. Rosemary West's defense was that her husband had forced her to participate in the attack on Caroline and that the fact that she was an occasional prostitute with a taste for unorthodox sexual practices did not mean that she had participated in serial killing. A complication was that some prosecution witnesses had sold their stories to the media, thus raising questions about their credibility. But there was evidence, not the least from her daughter Anne Marie, that Rosemary was not a mere victim of her husband, but his active collaborator in sustained and violent sexual abuse. The jury found Rosemary West guilty and the judge recommended that she should never be freed from prison.

1 A photo of the cellar next door to 25 Cromwell Road, identical in layout to that of the Wests.
2 Fred West being taken from Gloucester magistrates court.

THE BOSTON STRANGLER

The first victim of the killer who became known as the Boston Strangler (alternative nicknames included the Sunset Killer and the Phantom Strangler) was Anna Slesers, a fifty-five-year-old woman of Latvian origin. She was found strangled and semi-naked. At first, police thought that she had been killed by a robber, but there was no sign of forced entry to the premises and a gold watch and other items of jewelry had not been taken.

A spate of similar murders followed, causing panic in the city of Boston. Initially, all the crimes seemed to bear the same signature: The victims lived alone or with other women in apartments and were strangled with items of their own clothing, tied with a distinctive knot; they were all sexually assaulted and their bodies left in exposed positions; the apartments were ransacked, but nothing seemed to have been taken. Police sought the advice of psychiatrists and although the term psychological profile was not then current, that is in fact what they were after. The initial advice was to search for a mother-hating psychotic, but the murder of two women in their twenties seemed to contradict the analysis of mother-fixation.

Uncertain as to how to proceed, the assistant attorney general in charge of the operation talked to a Dutch psychic, Peter Hurkos, who claimed that his telepathic brain might help. He supplied a detailed and convincing description of the Strangler, which matched a suspect, but who later proved to be innocent. The consensus of psychiatrists was that at least two killers were at work: one who favored older victims and one or more other men who were trying to make their crimes resemble those of the first killer and who might be "unstable members of the homosexual community." Dr. James Brussel took a different view: he believed in a single culprit, a paranoid

schizophrenic about thirty years old who was searching, through killing, to find his potency.

In February 1965, while in the state hospital after being arrested for rape, Albert DeSalvo had a conversation with a fellow inmate that suggested he was the Strangler. F. Lee Bailey, the other inmate's lawyer, was told the story. Bailey spoke to DeSalvo and, after DeSalvo had confessed not only to the eleven known Strangler murders but also to two others, Bailey informed the police. Brussel's profile matched DeSalvo in most respects but there was a lack of forensic evidence linking DeSalvo to the crime scenes. Bailey took on DeSalvo's case and managed to secure a plea bargain that meant his client was never tried for the murders; instead, he was charged only with earlier crimes and sent to prison for life. DeSalvo had kept asking for medical help and Brussel believed that he was "simply and honestly bewildered by his own nature." But DeSalvo was transferred to a maximum security jail rather than a mental hospital. He was stabbed to death in 1973, and his own murderer has never been identified.

A photograph of DeSalvo, taken by the Cambridge police department.

SOUTHSIDE STRANGLER

The first victim of the so-called Southside Strangler in Richmond, Virginia, was Debbie Davis. Her body was found on September 17, 1987, in her apartment. She had been raped and strangled. Three more victims followed during the next three months.

A noticeable feature of the crimes was that they appeared to be signature killings. There were no fewer than thirteen points of similarity between the different killings. For example, each of the victims had apparently been overcome while asleep; there was no sign that a weapon had been used to subdue them. In each case, entry to the house was made through a window. Each victim had a stocky build. Each was killed by strangulation, and each had her hands tied. In each case, the murderer had tried to hide or partly cover the body before leaving and each crime occurred on a weekend.

A detective at the scene of the fourth killing noted a similarity between the killer's MO and that of a burglar he had encountered some years earlier, a man named Timothy Spencer, who took pleasure from breaking into homes when the occupants were sleeping. Investigators decided to interview him. When he was asked to provide a blood sample, Spencer asked if it was "anything to do with the rape": but rape had not been mentioned.

DNA profiling had recently arrived in the U.S. and had led to the arrest of a rapist named Tommie Lee Andrews. The Southside Strangler case was to be the first murder investigation in American history in which genetic fingerprinting of the prime suspect played a crucial part. Laboratory testing of Spencer's DNA sample provided a genetic match with a dried semen sample recovered from the body of the last victim, Susan Tucker. According to the scientists, the odds against a duplicate match in the DNA profile were 135 million to one. Later tests on two other victims also revealed a DNA match, although there was insufficient DNA material from the fourth victim to make a comparison.

When Spencer was tried for the murder of Susan Tucker, the defense called relatives of Spencer as witnesses, claiming that since they all shared the same genetic make-up, any of them could have provided a DNA match. The prosecution responded by threatening to introduce evidence linking Spencer to the other crimes, and the defense, realizing that such evidence would guarantee a conviction, did not pursue the "blood relatives" argument. Spencer was found guilty of first-degree murder and was later convicted of killing the two other victims whose bodies yielded damning DNA evidence. Coupled with the circumstantial evidence of Spencer's "signature," genetic profiling provided compelling evidence of his guilt and after several appeals failed, he was executed in 1994.

A DNA sample that can be used in evidence to prove that a killer was at a crime scene, as was the case with Spencer.

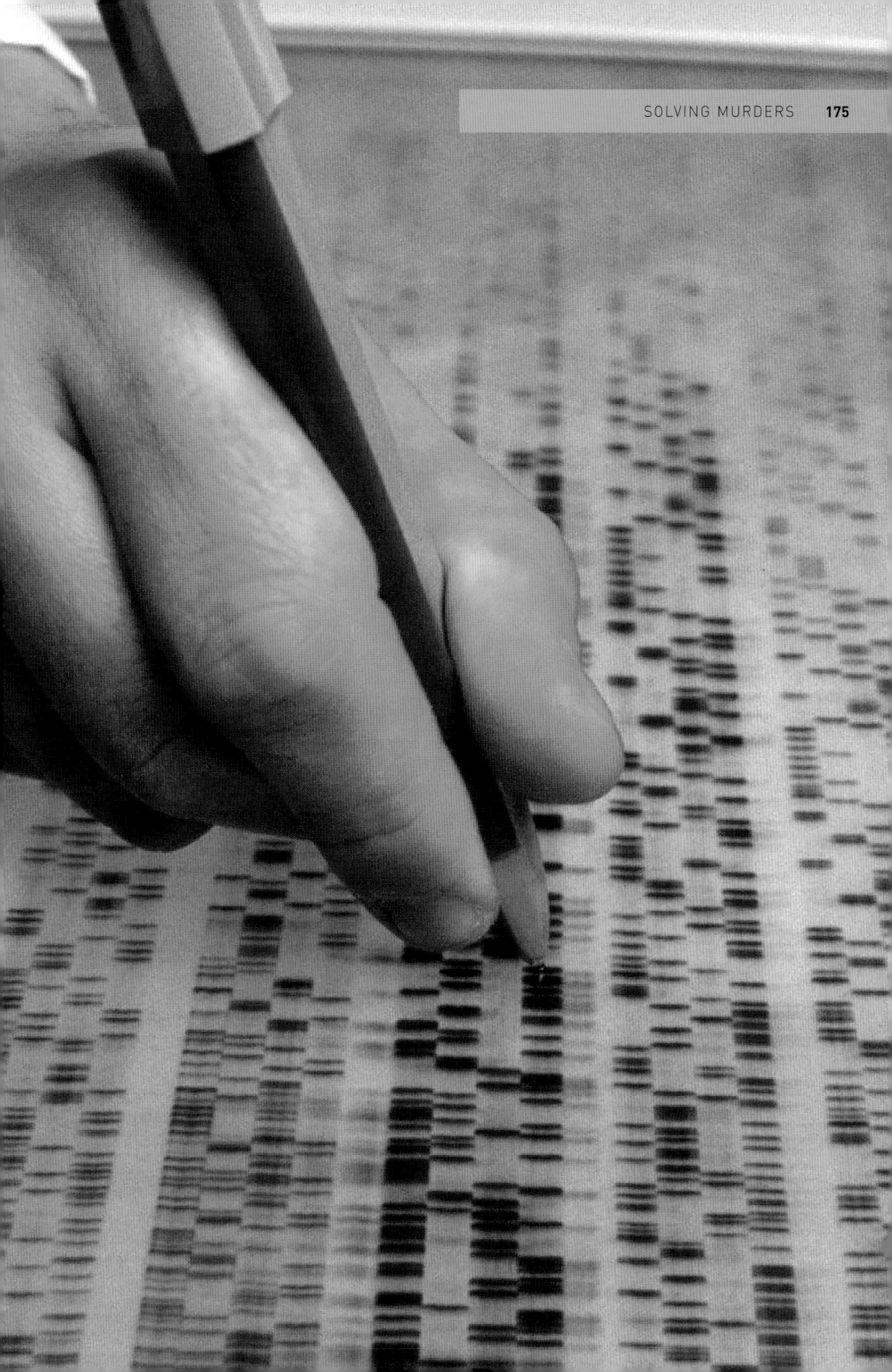

WRONGFUL IMPRISONMENT

The nine-year imprisonment and subsequent pardoning of Arthur Thomas illustrates the importance of forensic evidence in many murder investigations, and the need to take the most scrupulous care with such evidence. In June 1970, Harvey and Jeanette Crewe, who farmed at Pukekwa on the North Island of New Zealand, disappeared. Jeanette's father found his eighteen-month-old grandson in his crib in the farmhouse. The child was alive, and seemed to have been fed properly despite having apparently been left alone in the building for five days. However, there were bloodstains at the scene and a hunt for the missing husband and wife was put in motion, with the police having support from the military.

After a month, Jeanette's body was found in the Waikato River. She had been shot in the head with a .22 rifle and wrapped up in sheets that were then bound with wire. A few weeks later, her husband's body, which had been weighted with a car axle and dumped in the same river, was also discovered. He had been shot with the same weapon. Bullet fragments were recovered from the corpses and police established that there were two rifles in the local area that could have fired those bullets. One was owned by another farmer, Arthur Thomas, who was a former boyfriend of Jeanette. He had no satisfactory alibi and the police believed that the car axle had come from a trailer owned by the Thomas family. Wire similar to that used to tie up the bodies was found on the suspect's farm, while a cartridge case from his rifle turned up in the Crewes' garden.

Thomas was tried at Auckland's Supreme Court in 1972 and found guilty of both murders. He was sentenced to life imprisonment, but following a campaign in his support, he was granted a retrial in 1973. During the retrial, a friend of Harvey Crewe who had helped with the police search claimed that the area where the cartridge case was found had been searched previously, with no results. The police had had Thomas's rifle in their possession twice and the defense suggested that it would not have been too difficult to falsify the ballistics evidence. A leading forensic scientist suggested that Thomas's ammunition could not be connected with the bullets that killed the Crewes. The second jury also returned guilty verdicts, but the campaign on behalf of Thomas continued and ultimately a Royal Commission of Enquiry was asked to look into the case. The Commission decided that the cartridge case found in the garden had been planted there deliberately to cast suspicion on Thomas. He was pardoned and the government paid him a substantial compensation for the nine years he had spent in jail. No one else has been convicted of the crimes. One theory is that one of the Crewes shot the other and then committed suicide—but even this would have required a third person to dispose of the bodies.

An assault rifle of the type allegedly used by Thomas to commit murder.

CHAPTER FIVE

MURDER INSPIRED BY FICTION

> ## "It is the difficulty of the police romance, that the reader is always a man of such vastly greater ingenuity than the writer."
>
> Robert Louis Stevenson, *The Wrong Box* (1889)

The question of whether authors have a moral responsibility for their work is especially acute in the case of crime writers. It is from time to time suggested—especially in the more sensationalist news media—that particular crime novels have inspired criminals to commit murders, or at least to commit them in a particular way. Inevitably the truth is usually much more complex than the headlines suggest.

The first case of murder allegedly inspired by crime fiction occurred in Berlin in 1881. The hanged bodies of a woman and her five children were found in a locked apartment in a tenement block. At first glance it looked like the woman had strangled her children and then committed suicide. Her husband, a driver named Conrad, was apparently distraught, and the motive for the deaths appeared to be despair born of poverty. Soon, however, it emerged that Conrad had been having an affair and his mistress wanted him to leave his family. He attempted to commit the perfect crime by killing his wife and children, leaving the flat, and closing the door behind him. Previously, he had bored a small hole above the bolt and threaded through a thin piece of twisted horsehair: one end was attached to the handle of the bolt so that, by pulling from the outside,

A still from the film *The Hound of the Baskervilles* starring Peter Cushing as Sherlock Holmes.

Previous page: A body in the mortuary awaits examination by pathologists.

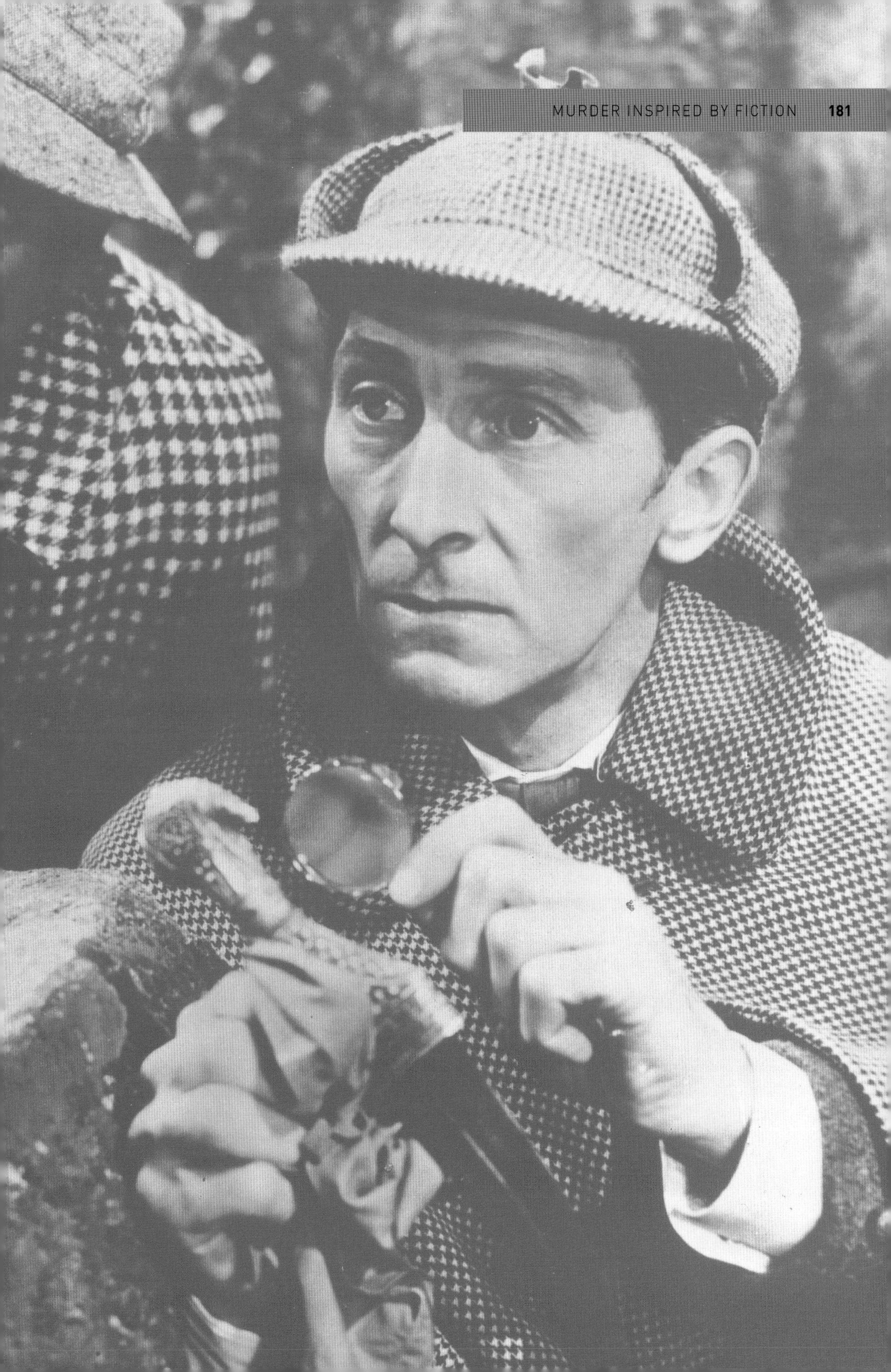

Conrad could draw the well-greased bolt home. He then jerked the twisted hair and most of it came through the hole so that he could remove it. He later filled the hole in the door with putty the same color as the door itself. Detectives also discovered that he was an avid reader and that he had come across *Nena Sahib* (1858) by Sir John Retcliffe (the pen name of Hermann O.F. Goedsche). The book is an early example of a locked-room or impossible mystery, about an Indian nobleman found dead in a room in London that is bolted from the inside. The culprit draws the bolt home from the outside by using a thin wire placed in a small hole in the door.

In 1929, the Australian crime writer Arthur Upfield, creator of the half-Aborigine detective Napoleon Bonaparte, was toying with an idea for his fourth novel. The story needed the body of a murder victim to be destroyed in such a way that the remains were not identifiable. Unsure as to how to achieve this in the context of his story, Upfield discussed his problem with acquaintances over a poker game. The plan that emerged from the conversation was that the victim should be taken into the bush, shot, and burned on a wood fire. The culprit should return to the scene of the crime a couple of days later and sift through the ashes, taking out every metal object and piece of bone remaining and destroying them. Kangaroo carcasses would then be burned over the ashes to conceal the true significance of the fire. A bush worker who took part in the discussion, John Thomas Smith, who used the alias of Snowy Rowles, was charged in 1932 with the murder of Leslie Brown. At the inquest, Upfield gave evidence explaining how Rowles had become aware of the method of concealing murder that seemed to have been copied in an unsuccessful attempt to hide the killing of Brown. By this time, Upfield's book, *The Sands of Windee*, had been published. Upfield gave evidence at the eventual trial, although Smith's lawyer argued that the novelist's testimony was irrelevant and the judge seemed to agree. Smith was found guilty and there is little doubt that, using a method based on the idea featured in Upfield's story, he killed two other men for personal gain and tried to conceal his crimes in the same way. His mistake was to allow himself to be linked to the victims, to fail to destroy the corpses completely, and to keep items that connected him with the dead men.

Crime writers have become increasingly meticulous in their research. The risk they run is that their fiction may provide practical guidance for would-be killers. In Frederick Forsyth's best-seller *The Day of the Jackal* (1971), an assassin's plot to kill the President of France involves obtaining a passport and false identity by using the birth certificate of a dead person. This simple yet potentially effective idea has been used on a number of occasions by real-life killers, but whether their planning has included a study of Forsyth's fiction is uncertain.

Often, the connection between a homicide and its supposed fictional inspiration is tenuous, if not downright incredible. In 2000, journalists claimed that an English pharmacist accused (and eventually convicted) of murdering his girlfriend with cyanide was inspired by the novels of Agatha Christie and Colin Dexter. In giving evidence, however, the pharmacist, John Allan, merely said that all that he knew about the effects of cyanide on the human body was "what everyone learned from films, Agatha Christie, and Colin Dexter books." A suggestion that a murderer in Florida gleaned helpful information from Patricia

1 The Polish born author, Joseph Conrad.
2 Agatha Christie, possibly the world's best known murder mystery author.
3 Cover of *Criminal Shadows* by David Canter.

INSIDE
THE MIND
OF THE
SERIAL KILLER

CRIMINAL SHADOWS

DAVID CANTER

BRITAIN'S PIONEERING
EXPERT IN
PSYCHOLOGICAL
PROFILING

Cornwell's debut novel *Post Mortem* (1991) seems equally far-fetched. Another unlikely suggestion is that Sir Arthur Conan Doyle, who was a doctor, poisoned Bertram Fletcher Robinson, who gave him the idea for *The Hound of the Baskervilles* (1901) and with whom he originally intended to write the story, simply to conceal the extent of Robinson's contribution to the manuscript. Mark Chapman, who shot John Lennon to death in New York in 1980, was reading J. D. Salinger's *The Catcher in the Rye* (1951) when he was arrested, but although Chapman identified with Holden Caulfield, the hero of the novel, that's a far cry from establishing that the book inspired him to kill.

When Ted Kaczynski, the Unabomber, was arrested, investigators noted a number of parallels between Kaczynski's murderous campaign and the behavior of the professor in Joseph Conrad's novel *The Secret Agent* (1907). The unkempt appearance, anarchistic views, and sense of injustice of the professor seemed to have echoes in Kaczynski's own life. But media suggestions that Conrad's writing inspired Kaczynski again seem greatly exaggerated.

Agatha Christie's novel *The Pale Horse* was first published in 1961. The book features black magic and the use of a poison seldom encountered in the pages of crime fictions—thallium. A few months later, fourteen-year-old Graham Young poisoned his stepmother with thallium. He was sent to Broadmoor, but following his release he poisoned eight more people, again with thallium. Christie's novel was mentioned at Young's trial by a pathologist who had consulted it as one of the few book descriptions then available of the nature and effects of thallium. Young's sister thought it likely that he had read the novel shortly after its publication, although Young himself denied it. Christie refused to comment on the possibility that her story might have assisted a killer, but her husband made it clear that she would have been deeply distressed had that been the case. The profiler John Douglas recounts in *The Anatomy of Motive* the case of George Trepal, convicted of murdering a neighbor by using thallium; a search of his home by the police and FBI uncovered various books on poison and also a copy of *The Pale Horse*. It is also worth noting that in 1975 Christie received a letter from a woman in Latin America saying that she had uncovered the attempted poisoning of a man by his wife, using thallium, as a result of reading the book. Shortly after Christie's own death, a nurse who had read *The Pale Horse* helped to save a child's life by recognizing the symptoms of a previously undiagnosed illness from descriptions in the book.

Responsible crime writers often take precautions to make sure that they do not inadvertently help potential criminals. In a note at the end of his book *Thin Air* (1994), which utilizes a clever method of murder, the British author Gerald Hammond explains his initial doubts about whether he should write the book. In deciding to do so, he took into account the fact that the relevant plot device had already been mentioned in literature available to the public. Hammond's approach seems reasonable and realistic. The main risk arises where a crime writer has specialized know-how of an unusual way of committing or concealing a homicide. It is absurd to suggest that crime fiction persuades otherwise law-abiding citizens to commit offences. Provided crime writers take sensible precautions in their accounts of murder techniques they can be acquitted of influencing criminal behavior.

Mark Chapman, the man who assassinated
John Lennon in 1981.

IT'S IN THE DRINK

Graham Young's murderous career had two distinct phases. As a boy of fourteen his enthusiasm for chemistry led him to become fascinated with poisons and their effects on the human body. He started to administer small doses of poison to members of his family in their food and drink and even when his stepmother died, he continued to do so until he was arrested. He was sent to Broadmoor special hospital for mentally ill offenders in 1962.

On his release in 1971, Young found a job with a photographic instruments firm. A few weeks later the head of the storeroom, Bob Egle, was taken ill and within eight days he was dead. Death was certified as due to bronchial pneumonia together with polyneuritis and an inquest was not considered necessary. However, more workers in the company fell sick. The next to die was Fred Biggs, head of the distribution department. Seven different doctors who examined Biggs during his six days in the hospital could not determine what was wrong with him other than a form of serious nervous complaint. Possible explanations ranged from the ridiculous—medieval-type plagues and evil spirits—to the plausible: a contaminated water supply or poisoning by radiation or heavy metal such as thallium, which is used in the manufacture of high refractive index lenses such as those made at the factory. Inquiries established that thallium was not used in the business and the favorite explanation was some kind of strong but unknown virus.

Graham Young attended a meeting of the whole workforce to discuss the problem and suggested that the victims' symptoms resembled those of people poisoned by thallium. Suspicion belatedly fastened on Young, and when the police arrested him and searched his bedroom they found not only poisons but also books about forensic medicine.

As in 1962, Young was quick to confess. He explained that thallium was his chosen method of murder. It is a poison whose effects are cumulative, causing death if enough small doses (not fatal in themselves) are administered over a period of time. Typical symptoms include loss of hair, scaliness of the skin, stomach pains, sickness, and loss of control of the limbs leading to paralysis and hallucinations. As Young correctly said to an investigating officer: "there are few doctors in this country who can identify thallium poisoning."

Yet thousands of crime fiction readers, given the symptoms of Young's victims, could have made an accurate diagnosis, thanks to the carefully researched descriptions of the effects of thallium in Agatha Christie's *The Pale Horse*. Christie, who had working experience as a nurse, had wide-ranging knowledge of poison and scientific accuracy was a feature of the novel (in which an early clue to the use of thallium is planted when a character's hair comes out with unusual ease). Young did not admit to basing his crimes on Christie's story, although his sister suggested that he had read it.

Young died in prison in 1990 at the age of forty-two. The cause of death was given as a heart attack—but speculation that he found a characteristically ingenious way of poisoning himself is, although entirely unproven, certainly intriguing.

Slough. G.I.E.

Slough. G.I.E.
Bath Road,
Slough.
April 28th 1971.

Mr. Foster,
Newhouse Laboratories, ltd.,
Bovingdon.
Dear Mr. Foster,
Thank you for your letter
of the 26th inst., in which you offer me
the post of asst. Storekeeper.
I am pleased to accept
your offer, and the conditions attached
thereto, and shall, therefore, report for work
on Monday, May 10th, at 8.30 a.m.
May I take this opportunity
to express my gratitude to you for offering
me this position, notwithstanding my
previous infirmity as communicated to you
by the Placing officer. I shall endeavour
to justify your faith in me by performing
my duties in an efficient and competent
manner.
Until Monday week, I am;
Yours faithfully,
Graham Young.

1 A copy of the letter written to Mr Foster of
Newhouse Laboratories Ltd, Bovington, by
Graham Young, accepting a job as an assistant
storekeeper.
2 Self portrait of a killer: Graham Young.

THE LANGUAGE OF MURDER

It helps to add authenticity to a crime novel featuring homicide detectives if the book contains a smattering of the slang that would be used by those detectives in real life. This is treacherous ground for authors, however, since slang is imprecise, dates quickly, and can vary from one part of the country to another, as well as between different countries. Sensitivity is required in the writer's use of slang in dialogue, since much slang can be offensive to minority groups. The same word or phrase can have quite different meanings from one place to another and drug cultures have generated a bewildering variety of terms used by those in the know. World wide broadcasting of American films and television shows about crime has increased familiarity around the globe with phrases, but there is no substitute for an author undertaking direct research with law enforcement officers in the jurisdiction where the story is set. With that in mind, here are some terms and acronyms commonly encountered, together with their most usual meanings.

ADW assault with a deadly weapon

AKA also known as

APB all points bulletin

B&E breaking and entering

BOL be on the look out for

Bus ambulance

BUST arrest

CI confidential information

DEALER person selling drugs

DOA dead on arrival, or deceased person

DOJ Department of Justice

DUI driving under the influence

DWI driving whilst intoxicated

EYEBALL to conduct surveillance,
   or the law officer who conducts surveillance

GOA gone on arrival, or leaving

ID identification

JDLR just doesn't look right
   (example of detective's instinct)

JOHN DOE, JANE DOE, JUAN DOE
   corpse of unknown identity
   (male, female, Latino)

MAIN MAN prime suspect

MIRANDA warning, prior to interrogation,
   to suspects of right to remain silent etc.

MO method of operation, modus operandi

NFD no further details

OD overdose

OP observation point

OWN GOAL criminal who kills himself
   or herself in course of committing crime

PERP perpetrator, criminal

PLAYER suspect

QT secret

SOP standard operational procedure

STAKEOUT watching suspect from
   a hidden location

SWAT Special Weapons And Tactics

TAIL follow a suspect

UTL unable to locate

WILCO will comply (with instruction)

WT walkie talkie

FURTHER INFORMATION

There is a vast array of books covering, in more detail, the subjects touched upon in this guide. The following is simply an introductory selection, with the emphasis on general texts. In addition, most notable murder cases have generated at least one book devoted to study of a particular crime.

Russell Bintliff, **Police Procedural**, Cincinnati,
   Writer's Digest, 1993

David Canter, **Criminal Shadows**, London,
   Harper Collins, 1994

D.J. Cole, **A Writer's Guide to Police Organization
   and Crime Investigation and Detection**, London,
   Hale, 1996

Mauro V. Corvasce and Joseph R. Paglino,
   **Modus Operandi: a writer's guide to how
   criminals work**, Cincinnati, *Writer's Digest, 1995*

Oliver Cyriax, **The Penguin Encyclopedia of Crime**,
   London, *revised edition, 1996*

John Douglas and Mark Olshaker,
   Journey into Darkness, New York, *Scribner, 1997*

John Douglas and Mark Olshaker, **The Anatomy of
   Motive**, New York, *Scribner, 1999*

Zakaria Erzinclioglu, **Every Contact Leaves a Trace**,
   London, *Carlton, 2000*

J.H.H. Gaute and Robin Odell,
   Murder "Whatdunit", London, *Harrap, 1992*

J.H.H. Gaute and Robin Odell, **The New Murderers'
   Who's Who**, London, *Harrap, revised edition 1989*

F. Tennyson Jesse, **Murder and its Motives**,
   London, *Pan, revised edition 1958*

Robert D. Keppel and William J. Birnes,
   Signature Killers, New York, *Pocket Books, 1997*

Brian Lane, **The Encyclopedia of Forensic Science**,
   London, *Headline, 1992*

Brian Lane, **The Encyclopedia of Women Killers**,
   London, *Headline, 1994*

Brian Lane and Wilfred Gregg, **The New Encyclopedia
   of Serial Killers**, London, *revised edition 1996*

Michael Newton, **Armed and Dangerous**,
   Cincinatti, *Writer's Digest, 1990*

Robert K. Ressler and Tom Shachtman, **Whoever
   Fights Monsters**, New York, *St Martin's Press, 1992*

Ann Rule, **The Stranger Beside Me**, New York,
   W.W. Norton, 1980

Carl Sifakis, **Encyclopedia of Assassinations**,
   New York, *Facts on File, 1993*

Serita Deborah Stevens and Anne Klarner,
   Deadly Doses, Cincinnati, *Writer's Digest, 1990*

Julian Symons, **Crime and Detection**, London,
   Studio Vista, 1966

Ronald R. Thomas, **Detective Fiction and
   the Rise of Forensic Science**, Cambridge,
   Cambridge University Press, 1999

Roger Wilkes, editor, **The Mammoth Book
   of Unsolved Crimes**, London, *Robinson, 1999*

Colin and Damon Wilson, **A Plague of Murder**,
   London, *Robinson, revised edition 1995*

Colin Wilson, **Written In Blood: a history
   of forensic detection**, London, *Equation, 1989*

Anne Wingate, **Scene of the Crime**, Cincinnati,
   Writer's Digest, 1992

Douglas Wynn, **The Limits of Detection**, London,
   Warner, 1992

Douglas Wynn, **On Trial for Murder**, London, *Pan, 1996*

Douglas Wynn, **The Crime Writer's Handbook**,
   London, *Allison & Busby, 1997*

Douglas Wynn, **The Crime Writer's Sourcebook**,
   London, *Allison & Busby, 2000*

WEBSITES

One of the glories of the internet is that the availability of effective search engines and good links, which abound on many crime-related sites, means that a wealth of research material is never more than a few clicks away. Here are a few of the thousands of possible starting points for further exploration.

The FBI: **www.fbi.gov**

Interpol: **www.interpol.com**

Crime Scene Investigation:
   www.crime-scene-investigator.net

Case Studies etc: **www.crimelibrary.com**

Page numbers in italics refer to captions